HIDDEN TREASURES
OF HERM ISLAND

by Catherine Kalamis

The Complete Guide to the Island's History

HIDDEN TREASURES
OF HERM ISLAND

© Catherine Kalamis

Publisher Wood of Herm Island

First published 1996
Reprinted 2013

ISBN 0 9527773 0 4

Originally printed and bound in Guernsey by
GP Printers, Guernsey, Channel Islands

Book scanned and recreated by Michael Walsh
at the Better Book Company, Chichester

Reprinted by Ashford Colour Press, Gosport, Hampshire

CONTENTS

Introduction

About the author

Catherine Kalamis has lived on Herm with her family since November 1991. She moved to the island with her Greek born husband and their two young children, then aged two and five, after many years of living in London.

Born in Surrey, Catherine longed for a country lifestyle as a young girl. Living on Herm has therefore fulfilled one of her earliest ambitions. She is a journalist and writer, and this is her second published book.

ACKNOWLEDGEMENTS

My thanks to:

All the helpful staff at the Priaulx Library, La Société Guernesiaise, Dr. Stanley Kellet Smith, Major Peter Wood, Adrian and Pennie Heyworth, Prof Richard Coates, Bob Burns, Jill Kendrick, Sheena and Nick Ie Messurier, Rachel Rabey, Heather Sebire, Tony Grange, Carel Toms, Griff Caldwell, The Island Archive Service, Michael and Andrew Dean, Brian Owen, Dr. David Shayter, Countess Lydia Blücher, The Estate of Sir Compton Mackenzie, The Ford Motor Company, The Society of Authors, Tim Thompson for kindly allowing me to reproduce his wonderful works of art on the front and back covers, and last but by no means least special thanks to Babis, George and Nikki for simply being there.

This book is divided into sections. At the end of each section there is a check list of landmarks, places, buildings or objects of interest which can be found on the island and are associated with the relevant era. Dotted throughout the book are fact boxes containing helpful information.

This book also includes carefully illustrated walks highlighting the island's historical past, and explaining the significance of some of the landmarks, as well as an introduction to some of the present day attractions – the beaches, plant and birdlife.

Readers Note:

Rosière – this name has evolved and is now also spelt Rosaire.

DEDICATION

In memory of Cathy, who made our life on Herm
a dream come true.

We will always remember the happy memories
of our time as a Herm family.

Babis, George and Nikki.

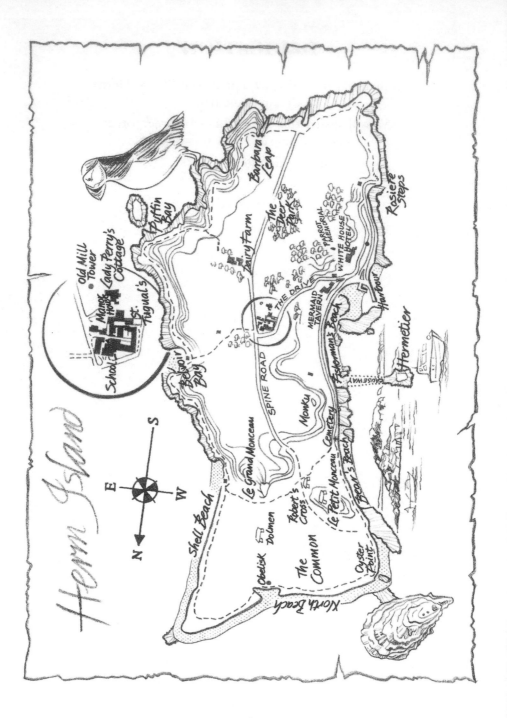

INTRODUCTION

"O Shell Beach, O Shell Beach,
Though daylight dies and night falls fast,
The hiss of waves will ever last ......"
– Shell Beach by Charles Clairmairis.

The island of Herm is a unique haven for thousands of visitors and holidaymakers from all corners of the globe, an idyllic natural playground in the heart of the Channel Islands. It is also home to 55 permanent residents who work in the 23 varied jobs required to keep the island open all year round.

This happy existence is, however, just one chapter in the island's long and colourful history, a mere snapshot in time. The Herm of today is quite different to bygone eras, when the island was mostly closed to the general public and great efforts were made to harness her assets in other ways, apart from tourism.

A cast of intriguing characters have left their mark on the island over the centuries. From the documents, letters and stories left behind it is clear that many were touched by the very special atmosphere that still exists on the island, one that is hard to find elsewhere.

Over the generations the island has been used as a monastic centre, a grand private estate, the source of artistic and literary inspiration, and an industrial centre for granite quarrying and silver mining.

It has been home to monks, missionaries, entrepreneurs, farmers and fishermen, writers, historians, and a family of Prussian aristocrats. History reveals that life was not always easy for many of the previous occupants. At times living conditions were spartan and harsh. Pirates and pillagers raided the islands. Later, a series of tenants went bankrupt, others were forced to quit for reasons beyond their control.

A great variety of plans for the island have emerged over the centuries – from penal colony to Swiss style health and therapy centre – although none have been as successful as the natural and peaceful haven that has evolved today.

But each new enterprise has, over the centuries, added an extra dimension to the island's qualities, and it is all these elements which today help to create the whole unique experience which is Herm.

In quiet moments one can almost reach out and touch the past. There is true delight in enjoying the exact same seaviews from Shell Beach or Belvoir Bay which others centuries before must have also relished. Or allowing the imagination to let rip and conjure up pictures of the great ocean going galleons that moored in Herm to collect granite from the quarries; and their departure as their huge canvas sails billowed in the wind.

There is a sense of history to be gained from standing on the common at dusk and imagining the prehistoric settlers, the first people to live in communities on the island 2-3,000 years before the birth of Christ.

Such different lifestyles, such different times have been had on Herm. Life has ebbed and flowed over the years like the sea around the island – there have been many births as well as deaths recorded in Herm's history.

Above all the island has managed to capture the imaginations of many high spirited and charismatic characters who have been drawn to the island by opportunism, or to enjoy its atmosphere of peace and history. Few have written more eloquently about the island than Sir Compton Mackenzie, Tenant of Herm in the 1920s, and I am glad to have had permission to reproduce many of his words and descriptions. Herm has also played a part in the creation of a world famous marine artist Tim Thompson, who lived on the island in the 1950s and whose earliest inspirational memories are of the sea surrounding the island. He painted the works of art which portray Herm during the granite quarrying days and have been used on the front and back covers of this book.

Remains of all these fascinating and individual time spans still exist on Herm, physically linking the past to the present day. If you know where to look, and what to look for, the fascinating story of Herm's treasured past comes to life and with it an ability to understand and make sense of the magnetism and enchantment of this quite special place.

Catherine Kalamis.

A Walk Back In Time
The Earliest Visitors –
10,000 BC onwards

"Nobody who has not experienced the wonder of approaching a small island in a small ship can imagine the eloquence with which land speaks ... providing an indescribable sensation ..."
– extract from "Fairy Gold" by Sir Compton Mackenzie.

Mesolithic Times – the first 'day visitors' arrive.

The first people to set foot on Herm arrived in the Mesolithic Period between the years 10,000 and 8,000 BC, clambering ashore from primitive floating craft. They were hunter-gatherers visiting the island in search of food at a time when Herm was considerably larger, and covered with oak and alder trees.

The Mesolithic people, originally from France and Jersey, lived in bivouac style dwellings on what later became Guernsey and made forays out to Herm.

They are historically interesting, as the first day visitors to the island!

Neolithic and Bronze Age Times – The first settlers

The first people to make Herm their home arrived in boats hewn from tree trunks at about the same time as the Pyramids were being built in Ancient Egypt, around 3,000-2,000 BC. They were farmers and cultivated the land, formed village settlements, and domesticated animals.

Perhaps the idea of living on an island excited the imaginations of these pioneering Neolithic settlers in much the same way as it continues to inspire those who love islands today. They certainly had great pride in their surroundings and sought out Herm as a place to live.

Neolithic and early Bronze Age people settled in groups and the remains of these early villages still lie untouched, buried beneath the sandy plain to the north of the island known as The Common. A treasure trove of unexplored remains is preserved here, waiting for an archaeologist of the future to discover.

At this time many of the granite outcrops to the west of the island including Hermetier, off the west coast, and The Humps, islets off Shell Beach, were linked to Herm, making the shape of the island both wider and longer.

The shelving, rounded top of the island would have looked fairly similar to its present day appearance (but with fewer trees). Neolithic people chopped down trees with polished stone axes to make room for farming. The shoreline, however, would have been quite different, with unformed beaches and vegetation reaching down to the water's edge.

At one time Herm might have supported a community of about 500 people. These first settlers were part of a rapid spread of population travelling west from central Europe as far as Ireland, looking for areas to cultivate.

> *Small in stature, the Neolithic island settlers grew crops and reared animals such as pigs, sheep and goats and oxen. They grew wheat and rye in Herm and learnt to grind it between stones to make a form of bread. They also fished, and collected limpets from the rocks. The women wore beads and bracelets.*

The north end of Herm proved the best for growing crops and building dwellings, although there is evidence of a very early settlement at the top of the island, near the present day Manor Village.

Herm Island tribes respected their dead and used elaborate funeral rituals. Large numbers of carefully built burial chambers (known locally in the Channel Islands as 'dolmens') dating from this period have been found on Herm and can still be seen. Indeed, tombs from this period have survived better than the houses that were built for the living.

> *Menhir – a standing stone*
> *Dolmen - a local term for a chambered tomb, technically a passage grave or long grave*
> *Cist – a small stone burial area, usually the grave of one person*

Primitive forms of engineering were used to move the huge granite boulders, found everywhere on Herm, to build the tombs. The boulders were placed at the head or entrance to the burial chambers and as supports inside the graves.

Rough ropes were used to pull stones, or they were rolled or carried.

It would have taken time and considerable effort to carry them up the hills which surround The Common.

The remains

The north of the island holds the most accessible, and visible, remains from the Neolithic and early Bronze Age period.

The first archaeologist to excavate in Herm was the Victorian, Frederick Lukis, who started his exploratory work in 1837 but did most of the excavations in 1840 and 1841. Some of his earliest discoveries such as human bones, pottery and primitive jewellery can be seen in the Guernsey Museum in St. Peter Port.

Lukis discovered different types of tomb: burial chambers, which contained the remains of up to 30 individuals, and smaller tombs or cists which contained the remains of one or two people. Large and elaborate tombs might have been the resting place for leaders of the community. Remains of food and bowls were found in the tombs, indicating a belief in some form of 'after life'.

The shapes of the tombs are not uniform: some are large and circular, others rectangular with a large piece of granite standing upright at one end. There is no doubt they were all sacred, and deeply venerated.

It was once thought that Herm was a ceremonial burial ground used by communities from beyond the island. But archaeologists now believe that the tombs were, in fact, all linked to the settlements. The individual tribes of the time probably had their own different religions, based on what is now known as paganism, involving worship of nature and the environment.

The tombs found in Herm are, mostly, situated on the hilly parts of the island. It is extraordinary to think that beneath the horseshoe shaped formations of rocks, the tombs and physical remains of the very first islanders to settle on Herm still lie.

In a book about Jethou (the small privately leased island which lies off Herm) Group Captain W H Cliff, the 21st Tenant of Jethou describes an unusual capstone found on the island.

The stone has a hole through the top, made by an implement - it was discovered in Jethou's 'fairy wood'.

When he wrote the book in 1920 Cliff suggested that the large granite rock once stood directly in a line with two other unusual stones – the Gate Rock, another rock with an apparently man made hole through it which can still be seen on an islet opposite Rosière Steps, and a menhir which once stood above a Neolithic tomb overlooking Herm's North Beach, and out to sea towards the Humps and Casquet rocks beyond.

(This large granite standing stone was destroyed by quarrymen 150 years ago, and the obelisk, Pierre Aux Rats, was built to replace it to act as a marker for fishermen. Proof that the menhir existed lies on the page of a 15th century map of Herm, now in the British Museum)

Cliff suggested that these three stones ran in a line and might be evidence of some sort of early worship of stones 'in high places' or rituals connected with them.

There again it could just be coincidence; one of Herm Island's mysteries which will probably never be solved.

There is little doubt that the lives of these early settlers were influenced by the raw, natural beauty of the island. Stand at any of the tomb sites on the hills around the common and the island stretches out before you. Archaeologists believe that the leaders or most important personalities within the community were buried at these high points to 'watch over' the living.

It is at these sites on the the island that visitors today can experience the **full** power of the natural elements of sun, wind and rain just as the Neolithic settlers did 4,000 years ago.

Where to see the ancient remains

Sixteen ancient Neolithic and early Bronze Age sites have been identified in Herm. Details of the sites are contained in T.D. Kendrick's book *Archaeology of the Channel Islands*, in which he devotes 22 pages to Herm. He used Lukis's early notes to identify the tombs and burial sites.

Petit Monceau: This small hill is on the left as you cross the first part of the common from Fisherman's Path. There are seven tombs: one burial chamber and six cists or single graves, on the eastern, northern and western sides of Petit Monceau. Look for a horseshoe shaped set of stones on the flat topped shoulder of land midway up the eastern side of the hill - a number of human bones, including those of a child, were found here along with pottery, animal bones, and limpet shells.

Grand Monceau: There are five burial sites on this hillside. On a plateau below the top of this larger hill there is a 21 foot long burial chamber. This was first discovered by Lukis in 1838 and excavated in 1840. A large granite boulder was originally lain across the tomb, but this was probably vandalised by quarrymen searching for good sized granite blocks to cut for use for making railway lines and pavement curbs on the mainland. On the western side of this hill is the largest tomb, which contained the remains of between 20 and 30 individuals as well as a complete vase. There are further unexplored cists on the eastern and western parts of the hill, and the boulders today look simply like a confused mass of stones under bracken and brambles.

Monku: On the top of this hill lies a horseshoe shaped arrangement of stones. Here, Lukis recovered human remains in 1841 as he stopped quarrymen treading on two human skulls in their eagerness to cut two large burial stones at the head of the tomb.

Robert's Cross: is so named for sentimental reasons, rather than historical ones. A horse called Robert, owned by the Wood family in the 1950s, was buried near here.

The tomb is on the common, at the cross roads of The Spine Road and the path leading west towards Oyster Point. The burial chamber is clearly seen, dug out and open and it is possible to step down into the chamber, which is still partly covered by a capstone.

Lukis found a narrow door 18 inches wide covered by two small capstones. The holes were filled with rubble, effectively closing the tomb. A Roman tile was found here, as well as animal bones and fragments of pottery which suggests the first amateur archaeologist of this site may in fact have been a Gallo Roman visitor. On a second clearing of the site in the late 1800s a polished stone axe was found.

Another burial chamber, now overgrown, is situated at the foot of Petit Monceau to the left of Roberts Cross.

The Common: A pile of stones lies near the obelisk, Pierre Aux Rats, or Ratstone. These are often thought to be Neolithic remains but this is a mistake: they are merely workmen's rubble from the quarrying days when the labourers got to work on the large menhir which stood above North Beach.

The structure was demolished on the orders of Jonathan Duncan who ran the quarrying operations in the 1800s. The granite from this structure was sent to London to be used for the base of the Duke of York's column. As the granite company faced financial difficulties at the time, another supplier was finally preferred.

Oyster Point: A burial tomb can be seen above the beach but there are no records of any remains being found.

Other sites.

In 1845 a Neolithic burial site was found to the east of the Manor Village. In 1846, a gardener found a stone slab and two polished stone axes in a field near the Old Mill.

And in 1908 other sites, one in the south, another to the east of the island, were unearthed, although they are now overgrown.

The Iron Age.

The remains of Iron Age settlements dating from 500 BC to 200 AD lie intact beneath the sand blown plain of The Common - a host of hidden treasures. Chunks of attractive red pottery from this era have surfaced, as well as other pots and vases covered in haematite, a form of iron ore so symbolic of settled Iron Age communities.

The pottery may not necessarily have been made in Herm - by this stage in history the Channel Islands were on an important trading route for travellers from the Mediterranean, Spain and what is now Germany. Goods were exchanged, ideas picked up and new implements developed. The remains of red bricks, known as briquetage, used by people in the Iron Age to extract salt from sea water through evaporation, are still regularly discovered on the banks of Fisherman's Beach.

The Gallo Roman Period.

Some fragments of pottery from around 300 AD are the only clues that the colonising Romans passed through Herm. They did not settle here, as Herm was off the main trading route between Gaul and South east England but they certainly visited, maybe for some early rest and relaxation and to enjoy the beaches, which were, by now well formed and already beautiful! The Channel Islands were on the edge of the known Roman world but some of their civilising influences rubbed off on the local population.

Tiles and pottery from this era have been dug up around the island, as well as coins which are now in the Guernsey Museum. But no evidence has yet emerged of any Roman settlement or villas on the island.

To find out more about Herm's early history, and see some of the objects unearthed on the island, visit the Guernsey Museum in Candie Gardens. The British Museum also has some relics from Herm.

For further information about archeology tours of the island contact the Archaeology Section, La Société Guernesiaise, Candie Gardens, St Peter Port, Guernsey. Tel 01481 725093

*Neolithic and early Bronze Age burial tombs
around The Common

*Robert's Cross

*Obelisk marking the point of five ancient standing stones above
North Beach

*The Common, or sandy plain (evidence of lron Age settlements still
waiting to be unearthed in this area)

*The Humps and Hermetier, once linked to Herm.

* Grand and Petit Monceau and Monku, the hills around The
Common, where Neolithic tombs can be seen.

*The banks of Fisherman's Beach where Iron Age briquetage has been
recently found.

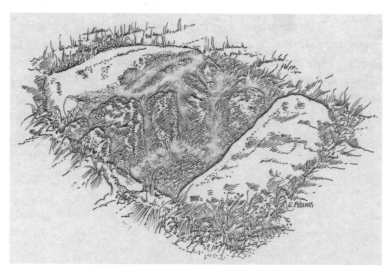

1 – A Neolithic burial site

Of Monks and men -
From 485 - 1569

"The gentle sunshine of an autumn day
Bathes the encircling waters ruffled by the breeze,
As upwards to this fair isle's hill top church through cloist'ring trees
The toilers of its farmlands wend their way"
– Charles Clairmairis

The position and solitude of Herm in mediaeval times held a spiritual appeal for the next set of residents on the island. A growing awareness of Christianity was nurtured in Herm by the monks and religious communities who settled on the island over many centuries.

Early Celtic Christian missionaries whose religion had an air of mysticism, and later different more orthodox groups of Norman monks, cultivated and farmed the island, kept bees, sought peaceful contemplation (sometimes in complete silence), gave religious instruction and worked on boat building.

The missionaries arrive

The island was visited by missionary monks in the sixth Century. They were from Wales and had initially fled to Brittany (known then as Armorica) to escape the tyranny of the Anglo Saxon invaders in their home areas. Amongst the refugees were St. Magloire, and a relation St. Sampson, who landed on the east coast of Guernsey at the site of the harbour which is still named after him, and which can be seen on a clear day from the west coast of Herm.

St. Magloire, on a missionary excursion, was granted part of Sark as a gift for healing an ancient Chieftain of the island. He established a colony of 62 monks on the island and they set about converting the local islanders, and established a foothold in Herm.

St. Magloire ran a strict order dishing out lashes for misdeeds, and frowned upon the islander's pagan rituals, such as worshipping the sun and dressing up as animals.

A story persists that St. Magloire's followers built a chapel on the Pierre Percee Reef, which lies off Rosière Steps, between Herm and Jethou, at a time when the water levels were lower and the area drier, although evidence for this is sketchy and inconclusive.

The Celtic Church was steeped in mysticism and spiritualism and the idea of building a church upon a rocky reef is a romantic one – it would certainly have been an obvious symbol to the plunderers and pirates who later plagued the waters around the islands but whether it really happened is not known. (History books say that a great earthquake hit Guernsey in 709 causing a tidal flood affecting the west coast – whether this natural disaster had any effect upon the little church, if it did exist, will never be known).

First building on Herm

There is little doubt that one of the first buildings on the island was a church or dwelling for these visiting monks, and all the indications are that the first stones were laid on the site of the present day Priest's Cottage, which is now used as holiday accommodation by visitors. It is next door to the chapel built and dedicated to St. Tugual, another missionary monk of the same era.

The Saint of Herm Island

St. Tugual, like St. Magloire, was born in Wales in about 490 AD. He too left his home area to seek refuge and free lands in Brittany. He came from a well respected family; his relatives included clan chieftains in south west England. St. Tugual was responsible for the creation and establishment of a religious group in Brittany and later became the Bishop of Treguier.

It is generally accepted that St. Tugual made several missionary excursions from his Brittany base and it is supposed that on one of these journeys he came to Herm and established a religious group.

Another theory is that it was the monks from his group who made the missionary journey alone and named a religious settlement after him.

It is not until 1251 that St. Tugual's name is officially linked to Herm in any form of ecclesiastical documentation. An ancient register of churches of the time lists a chapel dedicated to St Tugual on Herm but this was recorded some 700 years after the saint had died.

Although the detailed story of the island saint's life may be lost in the mists of time St. Tugual's missionary influence can still be felt in the calm and quiet of the peaceful St. Tugual's Chapel, situated in the Manor Village.

St Tugual's Chapel

The chapel today lies in the heart of the Manor Village, restored and cared for and still very much in use. Although the first religious house may have been built on this spot as long ago as the sixth century, the chapel as it exists today dates from later, between 1028 and 1035, and was built by Norman monks.

The design of the chapel is of interest: it was arranged so that the occupants of the nave were not visible to the main congregation. This is where the monks sat, out of sight of the lay congregation.

For some years in the 1800s the chapel was used only as a laundry. It was restored and reopened as a chapel by Prince Blücher, a tenant of Herm at the turn of the century.

Today, non denominational services are held most Sundays, and island residents may have their marriages blessed in the chapel. Special services are held at Easter and Christmas, and the children of Herm School perform an annual nativity play on the altar steps.

St. Tugual's Feast Day is December 1.

The Norman Monks' Rule 900-1542

From the middle 900s the Channel Islands, including Herm, came under the control of the Duchy of Normandy, which had a centralised seat of government in Rouen.

Herm was handed over by the Norman dukes to the control of various Norman monasteries which 'ruled' from different locations - namely Coutances, Mont St. Michel, and Cherbourg. (There was a short spell between 1199 and 1202 when the island's ecclesiastical affairs were controlled by the Parish of Exeter).

2 – St. Tugual's Chapel today

Between 1028 and 1035 Herm was given to the Benedictine Abbey of Mont St Michel by Duke Robert of Normandy and it was this group of monks that built the chapel and dedicated it to the memory of St. Tugual.

The monks established vineries on the island, farmed and gave religious instruction for 30 years. They were also granted the right to claim items washed up on the island from shipwrecks which happened regularly in local waters during the Middle Ages. Boats tackling the rocky unchartered waters would often sink, or passing vessels were attacked and destroyed by pirates. Booty would then be washed up upon the island's shores, often making a profitable sideline!

William the Conqueror (Robert's son) gave Herm over to the Augustinians of Cherbourg and another flourishing religious house was established which included a mediaeval carp pond. Local people were employed to help run the farm of cattle and sheep.

In 1480 the Prior of Herm was Jean Guyffard, who became an important local man, holding his own Court of Assize with judgment of life and limb. Centuries later a headpiece from a gallows was discovered on Herm which may have originated from this era.

The prior also had the right to any wreckage, or flotsam thrown up by stormy seas which swirled in winter around the island.

Franciscan Cordeliers, the Grey Friars who wore the famous grey gowns and twisted cord belts, settled in Guernsey and established an order in Herm. But they did not stay long because of the 'heathen nature' of passing bandits. All they wanted was some 'peace and solitude'.

Some of the unusual names of the fields of the island date from this time.

According to ancient manuscripts one Claude Panton described as the "Hermit of Herm" was present at the dedicaton of St Sampson's Church in Guernsey in the 10th century. It is thought that now lush and green Valley Panto was named after him.

Hard Times on Herm

Different groups of monks remained on Herm until the Reformation in the 1500s. During the ecclesiastical rule of the island Herm was probably shared with peasant farmers (who cultivated the fields with ox driven ploughs) and men on the run from the civil authorities.

Historians with a particular interest in Herm, suggest that the stone walls along The Spine Road, and around many of the fields, might have been originally laid with the help of men escaping from the harsh civil courts, who sought refuge and claimed 'immunity' on the island, which was governed by the separate ecclesiastical courts.

From the sketchy information we have of the time, it must have been a fairly rough and ready existence.

The islands were at the mercy of passing pirates, and Viking plunderers. It is likely that transient labourers would have proved useful, carrying out the hard work for the monks or even offering 'protection' in return for temporary refuge.

It would have been very tough work dragging, or carrying boulders for the dry stone walls which stand to this day along the Spine Road, one of the oldest, and straightest tracks, cutting across the island from The Common to the south coast.

By 1204 the Channel Islands were politically separated from Normandy, but Herm remained under the control of the Norman church for another 300 years. Because of its position in the Channel Islands, Herm was geographically at the centre of action between warring French and English armies during the Hundred Years War in the 1300s as the English and French kings battled for power.

Smoking cannons and explosive sea battles must have been witnessed from the shores of Herm. The island might also have come under attack from marauding French privateers. (A cannon is in place today in Herm Harbour, cemented upright into the stone walls and is used as a mooring point for boats).

Fighting went on in Jersey, Guernsey, Sark and Alderney - anyone living on Herm at the time must have had a bird's eye view as the French and English in turn fought and captured Castle Cornet, which was then contained on its own island stronghold.

In 1536 Henry VIII confronted the Bishop of Coutances over the islands. He urged all 'foreign friars' in Guernsey (and surrounding islands) to swear allegiance or face the consequences. It was at this stage the last Norman monks departed and sailed for France.

For a while the island became a paradise for passing pirates and villains. A historian of the time described Herm and Sark as "islands of thieves, banditti, picaroons, robbers, ruffians and murderers …"

On May 10th 1567 the Bishop of Coutances tried to exercise ecclesiastical rights for the last time to claim money from the island. He was unsuccessful. In 1569 Queen Elizabeth I handed Herm over to the ecclesiastical control of Winchester.

Soon Herm was to evolve again. In this transformation the island was to become an exclusive game reserve for the governors of Guernsey. The dwellings used by the monks became a 'lodge' for the gamekeepers employed by the high ranking Governors of Guernsey, representatives of the British Crown.

The Pierre Percee Rock

The rock is situated just across from Rosière Steps and may be seen on ferry crossings which pass through the Little Russell between Herm and Jethou.

Whether a chapel was really built in the 6th Century upon its harsh ground will forever remain a mystery – but what cannot be explained is an intriguing rock on this reef which stands opposite Jethou. Known as the Gate Rock, it has a hole through it – which is presumably how the rock derived its name (percee meaning pierced).

Various theories have been put forward as to the origins of this hole. It may, claim some, be the only remaining evidence of a chapel on the reef. It may have been made as a mooring for either Viking or Elizabethan vessels.

The story I like the best is the most unlikely, but the most romantic. This site, so the legend goes, was once a mermaid market – the long tailed ladies of the sea were tied to the rock and then offered for sale!

(With thanks to Dr. Stanley Kellet Smith, author of an article on The Pierre Percee Rock in the Guernsey Society Journal, 1960).

15

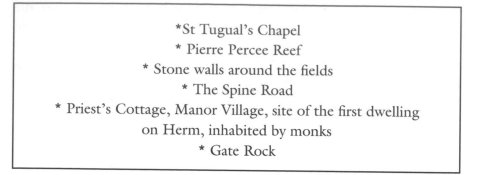

*St Tugual's Chapel
* Pierre Percee Reef
* Stone walls around the fields
* The Spine Road
* Priest's Cottage, Manor Village, site of the first dwelling
on Herm, inhabited by monks
* Gate Rock

3 – The interior of St. Tugual's Chapel

The Governors' Retreat 1570-1810

"Island of Erme, other Herme and Arme, with the house thereon erected formerly a chapel, and all the deer, partridges and rabbits ..."

– description of the island in 1737

The Governors of Guernsey, representatives of the reigning monarch, lived in grand style at Castle Cornet up until the year 1672, and enjoyed lovely views of Herm from the castle's east facing windows.

During the 16th and 17th centuries Herm Island became a private pleasure ground and game reserve for these wealthy, well connected Governors who took to sailing over to the island for hunting, shooting and fishing.

Sir Thomas Leighton was the first Governor who enjoyed the exclusive use of Herm as his private 'back garden' retreat during his term of office, between 1570 and 1609. He annexed the island as a game reserve stocking it with pheasants, swans (which were eaten at table), rabbits and partridges.

Leighton was governor of Guernsey for nearly 30 years, strict and puritanical, but a great lover of 'sport'.

(During his governorship for example, men and women accused of adultery in Guernsey were imprisoned for three weeks, and on Saturdays held up to public ridicule in a cage. The punishment also included 24 lashes 'until blood be drawn'.)

Despite the fact that pirates (including the infamous Barbary pirates) still sailed the local waters, Leighton regularly visited Herm on hunting trips, accompanied by high ranking friends, and relatives.

Although Herm was effectively a private island local people were able to travel over in their own small boats to collect 'vraic' or seaweed although in 1616 'strangers' were liable to be fined £10 if they were discovered taking part in this very local tradition. (Seaweed was and still is used as an excellent manure for cultivating fields).

Tragedy struck on one trip in August 1587. The Governor and a hunting party including his son and four young friends and their tutor Mr. Isaac Daubeny set off for Herm at dawn, in high spirits.

When they arrived on the island the boys settled down to lessons followed by singing for an hour and prayers. The boys were determined to enjoy themselves and wanted to go swimming after lunch. Tragically one of the boys, Walter St. John, found himself in trouble off Belvoir Bay, which at that time had a lot of long seaweed growing from its depths. The boy may have swum too soon after lunch for he lost his balance and was knocked over by a large wave. Mr Daubeny rushed to his rescue but he was also 'overcome'. They both drowned.

The Governor was said to have been overwhelmed with grief that such a happy day had ended with a tragic loss of life.

Herm continued to be a 'pleasure resort' for successive Governors through the next century, although many of them were 'absentee' officials and with the confusion of the Civil War may never have stepped foot on the island, governing in name only from the mainland! However, the facility was there if they so wished. (When the last governor left Castle Cornet after an explosion ripped through the building in 1672 Herm was still the governors' private island).

Herm certainly gave pleasure to the high ranking officials and their families. A glimpse of that time is given by Dorothy Osborne, the daughter of Sir Peter Osborne, who was appointed Governor of Guernsey in 1621. In a collection of her letters to her future husband she recalls the lovely island of "Arme" and the happy visits she made as a teenager. (See page 74 – Literary and Artistic Connections).

In 1629 Herm is described as *"neer three miles in circuit, a solitary dwelling once of canons regular ..... but now only inhabited by pheasants of which amongst the shrubs and bushes there are no scarcity"*.

In 1670 advocate Peter Gosselin hoped to start up a wool industry employing "200 persons in the knitting of the wool for the manufacture of stockings". He won permission to stock the island with sheep.

But his sheep farming days were numbered when the powers that be complained that the sheep grazing had caused the stocks of deer, and pheasants to be reduced by half.

Nearly 70 years later, in 1737, Major General Richard Sutton, then Governor of Guernsey, declared that he had no interest in keeping Herm or Jethou as a private reserve, and suggested that the islands be leased "in order to encourage persons to cultivate the land".

It was a sensible idea that appealed to King George II and his advisors as it meant another possible source of revenue for the Crown purse. In the official leasing document it was agreed that Sark people could continue fishing off Herm and collecting vraic "for the manuring of their land".

First Tenants of Herm

On May 21st 1737 Herm officially became a Crown owned 'fee farm' and was leased to the first Tenant of Herm, a Guernsey farmer Peter Carey. This first lease was issued for 61 years at the rate of £14 per year, renewable every 21 years for an extra payment of £42.

Carey was a hard working gentleman farmer. He complained about the law prohibiting the export of corn from Herm which also applied to Guernsey. Despite the restriction the farm continued to flourish and to ensure his tenancy he renewed the lease 11 years later.

He invested in the island, building a barn and stables and cottages in and around the present day Manor Village. The Old Mill Tower may date from this time.

In 1766 the first Tenant of Herm died but his son, also Peter Carey took over the island farm and was given permission to 'erect fences' as he expanded the farming interests.

Peter Carey the second died only four years later and the lease passed to a relative, Caroline Carey, who decided she had no use for the island. In 1737, during her brief ownership, the last deer, presumably left over from the previous era, were killed.

A year later Caroline Carey sold the lease to the de Jersey family who were also farmers. They opposed plans by the States of Guernsey to quarry stone from Herm to build a harbour extension. The family lost the case and in 1777 the first granite quarrying on Herm was carried out. This was to be a foretaste of Herm's industrial era, launched in earnest over 40 years later.

19

The first innkeeper of Herm

By 1800 the lease had passed on again to Pierre Mauger who, in a document dated 1810, is also described as an innkeeper – the first time that there is any record of an inn on the island.

He had a fairly troubled tenancy and took out various injunctions against people with a complaint against him one of whom described him as a 'damned thief, a damned rascal, and a damned smuggler' and then proceeded to beat him about the face with a stick!

Mr. Mauger fell on hard times and once more the lease of Herm changed hands. The island was about to enter one of the most historically fascinating time spans when it changed from rural farmland into an industrial centre for granite quarrying.

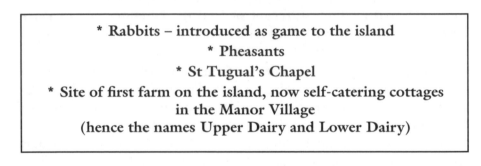

* Rabbits – introduced as game to the island
* Pheasants
* St Tugual's Chapel
* Site of first farm on the island, now self-catering cottages in the Manor Village
(hence the names Upper Dairy and Lower Dairy)

4 – An 18th century print of Herm – note the absence of trees on the skyline.

Quarrying and Scandal
on Herm 1815 – 1870

"Herm Island is proud that those steps of grey granite,
Were hewn from its cliffs, and a century old,
As staunch and unworn as their loyalty to England,
Will stay so, as long as her history is told"
– Herm Island to London Town, by Charles Clairmairis.

The Hon. Col John Lindsay, an heroic veteran of military campaigns in India and France, launched the granite quarrying industry in Herm.

But he originally bought the 21 year island lease to Herm from Pierre Mauger for quite a different purpose: as a home for his mistress and three children.

This arrangement – considered scandalous by standards of the day – had the blessing of Lindsay's aristocratic and elegant wife, Lady Charlotte North. She was the daughter of the Earl of Guildford, a lady in waiting to Queen Caroline, and had been married to Lindsay for 15 years, when he bought Herm.

Lady Charlotte accepted her husband's affair with dignity and tolerance. Not only did she know of his long relationship with Mrs. Colebrook Cooper, a widow from Bermondsey, but she also befriended her and visited her and the children in Herm. Maybe she thought that providing for them far from their society friends in London was the best solution. Lady Charlotte obviously had a great affection for Herm as she made many pen and ink sketches of scenes around the island (see page 23).

Sir Walter Scott met Lady Charlotte Lindsay in 1806 and writes about her in a letter: "Her wit flowed as if she was quite unconscious of it and always reminded me of a gifted princess who could not comb her locks without producing pearls and rubies."

It was extraordinary for a woman of her time to fully accept her husband's illegitimate children. But she was childless, and it is assumed that Mrs. Colebrook Cooper bore the Lindsay children Lady Charlotte was unable to have. As further evidence of this, Lady Charlotte became godmother to their first child, a daughter also named Charlotte.

Despite her acceptance of the relationship, Lady Charlotte must have been quite despairing of her husband. When Lindsay bought Herm he was in debt and had to borrow the money, £1,200, from her father to pay Pierre Mauger.

Lindsay's private affairs were as unorthodox as his business life which never quite seemed to come together in Herm following an heroic Army career. However, he became the man responsible for launching Herm's industrial age and put Herm on the map among London businessmen.

5 — Pen and ink sketches by Lady Charlotte Lindsay, which includes her signature.
The sketch shows the Farm House, Old Mill, dry stonewalls, and the two cottages
at the foot of The Drive – but no harbour.

The Hon John Lindsay, was 48 years old, with a distinguished military record with the 73rd Highlanders of campaigns in India and France when he put in a bid for Herm.

He was a born aristocrat, the ninth child of Lord and Lady Balcarres, who held an estate in Fifeshire. His sister Lady Anne Barnard was a confidant of both Sir Walter Scott and King George IV and one of his brother's Hugh Lindsay was director and chairman of the East India Company, and for many years had been a Scottish MP. Other brothers joined the Army serving in America and India.

Lindsay was one of only 14 soldiers out of his battalion to survive a massacre of British troops during the battle of Conjeveram in India and endured three years and 10 months of imprisonment by Hyder Ali between 1780 and 1784. He wrote graphically and emotively about these experiences in Vol III of the Lives of the Lindsays by Lord Lindsay a copy of which is held by the Priaulx Library in Guernsey.

Lindsay saw war action in France in 1793, quit the Army in 1801 and surfaced in Herm 14 years later. He was a desperate man when he bought Herm. Not only had he scandalised society by having an affair with a widow – it was in fact the continuation of a relationship he started before his marriage to Lady Charlotte – but he was also hugely in debt. Lindsay bought Herm as a refuge for his 'second family' and also in the wild hope of escaping from his ever encroaching creditors in London.

In one final attempt to escape debt he allowed his daughter Charlotte to 'buy' Herm's lease from him – the idea was to relinquish himself of his assets to escape his creditors. He never did escape from debt, and died bankrupt. However, in his favour, Lindsay's mistress (who had been disowned by her family) and their three children found sanctuary and peace in Herm and lived on the island happily for many years.

Dreams and schemes

After settling his children and mistress on Herm it took Lindsay a further six years before he opened the granite quarries. Until then Lindsay kept on the move, darting between the island (where he lived in the Farm House, now The Manor) and London thinking up how he could make money out of his island acquisition.

24

One of the most bizarre plans was a proposal to build a massive naval harbour on the east side of Herm (useful for stopping brandy smuggling from France, he maintained). Later he wrote to Sir Robert Peel suggesting he open a penal colony in Herm for 1,000 convicts.

Plans to start a Herm based lottery were made, then dashed, in a desperate bid to raise cash. His temper and 'violent language' became legendary as he desperately searched for the next money making scheme.

At one stage he inserted a long winded advertisement in the Gazette de Guernsey inviting subscriptions from rich and poor for £1,200 guineas to erect on one of the island hills "a mausoleum to the memory of King George II". He planned to use 3,000 tons of granite and ask a London architect to design the monument. Nothing came of it.

In 1820 he borrowed more money – this time from his brother, Lord Balcarres and employed a builder at 50/- a week to build three cottages in Herm. They may have been cottages at the foot of The Drive (which became known as the Keeper's Cottage) and Fisherman's Cottage, which appears in a drawing of the time.

Quarrying begins

When Lindsay finally decided to re open a quarry on the island he set about organising a stone landing area for picking up and dropping off the cargo. It was constructed from huge boulders – the original pier still exists as the curving pile of stones leading off the Hotel Beach directly in front of the White House Hotel and can be seen to the right of the photograph on page 30, one of the oldest of Herm, dated 1856.

Business began well enough and he set about marketing Herm granite in London for road and rail building. One of his first contracts was to supply stone for the maintenance of London Bridge.

As the contracts came in he recruited men from Aberdeen in Scotland paying the hard working and hard drinking quarrymen and stone masons 16/- a week and then charging 7/- a week for board and lodging. In London he organised a berth on Regent's Canal, Paddington to receive Herm granite. What a sight those great vessels must have been setting sail from the island with tons of heavy granite aboard.

6 - This picture was taken in either Guernsey or Herm at the time of granite quarrying depicting the workforce.

Herm granite was eventually used to construct steps in front of the Carlton House Terrace in Pall Mall in London, which are walked upon to this day, as well as curbstones, railway stones and pavement blocks in the East and West India Dock Roads.

In 1822 Lindsay wrote to Sir Robert Peel again, this time suggesting that 200 convicts were employed at a halfpenny a day to produce granite for the turnpike road. His Aberdeen workers, although tough, were expensive. His request was never met.

There was a growing interest in Herm granite but plenty of technical difficulties and Lindsay carried on spending money he did not have, buying cranes and other costly equipment.

He was enormously enthusiastic and forecast great things for the granite project telling the States of Guernsey in 1824 that he hoped the "entire granite trade of England and Scotland would become transferred to these islands".

He asked the States for a £1,500 loan to 'encourage local employment'. But the request was turned down (they must have been wary about this man with the big ideas) which is why, in November 1824 he entered into a business partnership with Jonathan Duncan, a wealthy London barrister and son of a Bombay governor.

7 – The Prison, Herm, which dates from the industrial quarrying era.

Duncan agreed to buy one third of all granite from Herm and take a share of the industry's profits in return for a loan of £1,500. Lindsay agreed to employ a further 20 workmen and 50 stonemasons and to provide accommodation for them on the island.

(The quarrymen lived roughly in dormitory style accommodation. The original Mermaid Cottage block was one set of living quarters. A room at a building on the site of the White House was used as a canteen). Although Lindsay and Duncan employed 400 workmen at the height of the industrial era, it is thought they worked in shifts, and that, at most 200 men stayed on the island at anyone time.

Jonathan Duncan

All too soon Duncan realised he had gone into business with a dreamer who failed to keep records or accurate accounts. Instead of cutting his losses, he revised the original agreement with Lindsay which, to his credit, included a safeguard for Lindsay's 'second family'.

Duncan secured contracts for the maintenance of Blackfriars Bridge in London, and for curb and paving stones for London streets.

8 – The Farm House, Herm circa 1856, one of the oldest photographs of Herm, courtesy of Mr. Michael Beaumont, Seigneur of Sark. (The present day Manor House).

The quarrymen were instructed to find large lumps of granite which could be cut neatly into blocks or squares (see photograph on page 26). The Neolithic dolmens were a perfect target as they stood straight and upright, and could be more easily cut.

Benjamin Wyatt, architect of the Duke of York's column in Pall Mall, London, tested Herm granite and found it twice as tough as granite from Cornwall. Wyatt wanted a block of this hard Herm granite for the base, and it was this commission that led to the destruction of the landmark dolmen above North Beach. When fishermen realised it had been pulled down they demanded an alternative land mark – the result was the obelisk, Pierre Aux Rats, which stands to this day, although the base is gradually becoming covered by wind blown sand.

It is ironic that the granite block was never used in the construction of the famous London monument. It probably had something to do with the financial difficulties that Duncan faced due to Lindsay's atrocious system of accounts that frightened off the architect at the 11th hour.

The beginning of the end

The strength of the granite was one of the reasons for the eventual downfall of the granite industry on the island.

Lindsay found that one man could only break up one and a half tons of granite a day and soon the great demand from England was for the perfectly adequate softer, and cheaper stone for railways and roads.

It was costly and time consuming to meet the orders and another major headache was the refusal by Lloyds to insure vessels sailing in and out of Herm with granite loads because of the treacherous currents. Only two years after signing up with Duncan, Lindsay died in London, bankrupt, owing over £5,000.

He had become a large man (he was buried in an 'outsized coffin') his physical size matching his extraordinary, determined and yet oddly charismatic personality.

Duncan lays the structural foundations of Herm

After Lindsay's death Jonathan Duncan married 20 year old Harriet, Lindsay's youngest daughter by Mrs. Colebrook Cooper, on February 12 1828 in Guernsey and then took over the lease of Herm. He was 49.

Duncan hoped to salvage some of his investment and was determined to get the island organised. More workmen were employed, and an assistant constable, James Hooper, sworn in to keep the peace amongst the hard drinking workforce.

It was around this time that the Herm jail was built, the beehive construction in the grounds of the White House Hotel which 150 years later was recognised by the Guinness Book of Records as the smallest prison in the world.

Despite his more ordered approach to the business Duncan's debts (which included some of Lindsay's) had risen to £12,700 by 1829.

Duncan poured money into the island. During his ownership of the lease he:

* installed two miles of road and track
* built the harbour in the position it stands today
* built more accommodation for the quarrymen in The Manor Courtyard area
* set up forges and a blacksmith's workshop
* built a brewery and bakery for the islanders

9 – The Mermaid Cottages, when they were used by miners. The large boulders to the right of the picture show the first primitive harbour extending out from the present day Harbour Beach.

Granite was hauled along what is now Fisherman's Path. (The Harbour Beach is referred to in old maps as "Sous l'haulage" which indicates it was used as a towing path for cart loads of granite hewn from Monku, Grand and Petit Monceau)

> *Buildings constructed during Lindsay's and Duncan's tenancies of Herm were: Harbour Cottage, Laranda, Foxglove, the Mermaid Cottages, Rosière Cottage, the original buildings which became the Mermaid Tavern, the original cottage that was later extended to become The White House Hotel, and a number of additional workmen's cottages in the area of the farm buildings, the present day Manor Village.*

Socially, the island population thrived; the quarrymen's families joined the workmen, and there were women and children to cater for.

It was around this time that the social reformer Elizabeth Fry wrote to Lord de Saumarez in Guernsey asking for his support to pay for a schoolteacher because Herm "has a considerable number of school children, no school, no place of worship and no religious instruction except the innkeeper (probably Lindsay's son John Colebrook Cooper who was described in a guidebook later as a worthy gentleman) reading them a sermon".

Nothing came of her proposal until 10 years later when the first schoolteacher, Rev Henry Benwell moved from Guernsey to Herm.

In 1829 Duncan formed the Herm Granite Company in partnership with a Geoffrey Martin, a businessman, and Ebenezer Fernie, an accountant.

But only a few years later he finally gave up trying to make any sort of profitable business from Herm granite and in 1837 was declared bankrupt owing thousands of pounds. He left Herm for Guernsey where he buried himself in a quite different pursuit – writing academic and historical books.

More changes on the island
In 1837 the lease of Herm was obtained by the British Commercial Insurance Company, managed by Ebenezer Fernie, who like Duncan and Lindsay before him, could see the opportunities and wanted to carry on quarrying.

He sub let the island to Peter Falla, a farmer who installed himself in the Farm House employing servants as well as labourers.

At this time day visitors enjoyed excursions to Herm known locally then as Herme. Shrimping parties were popular – visitors spent hours wading knee deep among the rocks to capture 'handfuls of shrimps'. Teas and wines were available for the visitors at the inn.

In an article dated 1838 a reporter says: "The place of rendezvous, or tap, and grocers shop is kept by Mr. Gay and a gay soul is he, and one universally respected!".

The visitors came ashore on fishing boats, steamers or opened topped wooden vessels. Then, as now, it was a family day out.

Twin interests in Herm

There were two distinct activities during the 1840s and 50s. Ebenezer Fernie was busy as 'overall manager' of Herm as well as trying to buck up the quarrying industry. He installed the railway crane and track made by Bray, Waddington and Co of Leeds which still stands as a landmark on Herm Harbour – it is dated by historians at around 1850.

(see page 34)

10 – This track is the present day Drive. Harbour Cottage, and the two cottages on the right, are among the earliest buildings which still stand on Herm.

A new company, the Hayter Granite Company, was formed. He employed families, and set up the first school for island children.

Peter Falla, meanwhile, looked after Herm's agricultural interests, farming the island's 300 acres for more than 10 years. He was appointed the constable of Herm in 1847.

Despite everyone's best efforts the granite business never became hugely profitable and soon quarrying operations were almost at a standstill.

Fernie carried on as leaseholder until 1854 by which time the island had been more or less abandoned by the small community of granite workers and the school was hardly in use.

The final death knell was the introduction of macadamisation of roads; Herm granite was simply not required.

The grocer takes over

Fernie's failures presented a golden opportunity for one of the longest serving islanders of his time – Stephen Martin Touzeau had lived on the island for over 25 years as the island grocer and as a boatman.

When Fernie decided to sell the lease in 1854 – 62-year-old Touzeau made a bid with a friend, Job Henry, and together they bought the lease of Herm for £1,500, each setting up a farm.

But their partnership and friendship ended in a sorry state – maybe neither man had the experience to manage an island. The pair became involved in an extraordinary contract which literally split the island in two, each man having set areas to call his own.

The men had quite different ideas; presumably they hoped to earn a living through farming, although Henry is described in one book as a beekeeper.

By 1860 the partnership was over, the two men must have been keen to sell, as they lost money on the lease, selling it on for just £1,000.

Stephen Touzeau returned to his old job as a boatman looking after some of the thousands of visitors who still enjoyed coming to Herm in the summer. One boatman of the time claims in a guidebook to have brought as many as 2,000 visitors to Herm during the summer for the beaches. Another guide of the time describes the steamers and ferries bringing visitors to the island. Rosière Steps had not been constructed and readers are informed that the "landing on the rocks is not pleasant for ladies or those unaccustomed to walking over rough boulders."

More attempts to make good

The next tenant was Thomas Bartlett from London, but his ownership lasted just two years. He was followed by John Thomas Hyde also from London who made another attempt to raise funds to re-open the quarrying. Hyde formed the second Herm Granite Company which was launched in London in March 1864 and planned to bring in 200 quarrymen. Shares in the company were offered in the local press.

Hyde commissioned the Island of Herm Granite Quarry print, a lithograph which depicts many of the features of the island and includes plans for a railway line link across the causeway to Hermetier as a PR exercise for his company.

He failed to attract enough interest in the company although he did manage to secure a good deal for future tenants, by arranging that harbour dues on ships in and out of Herm could be diverted towards the maintenance of the harbour.

Five years later he cut his losses and left. The lease was sold to the wealthy Lt. Col Montagu Joseph Feilden for £4,000, which was to also include the tenancy of Jethou.

The Herm Crane which stands on the harbour is of a type known as the Leeds Crane. The superstructure is built around a central pillar and was designed by crane builders in the Leeds area. With a wooden jib and cast iron side frame it is a typical, though fairly early, example of the many hundreds of hand cranes built in the Leeds area in the last century.

Originally loads would have been lifted by chain.

Interestingly, James Bray, a founder of the company, was a stonemason in Bradford and one of his early contracts was on part of the Leeds and Bradford railway line. His combined experience may have been the reason why the crane was commissioned from his company, for it was designed to run on a railway track and lift large loads of stone.

The Waddingtons of the company were railway contractors also on the Leeds area who also made the necessary heavy equipment for building railways.

In summary

The era which began with so much hope and enthusiasm ended with shattered dreams, and with huge debts for all concerned, as well as a fairly mangled island with blocks of uncut granite left in tumbled heaps. The granite industry destroyed many of the fascinating ancient relics on the island to the complete and utter fury of the acutely sensitive Victorian archaeologists and the island was in a complete mess by the time the last quarrymen sailed away.

It was down to Feilden to start a major clear up operation. As a man of wealth and character, he had the time and money to invest in the island, although history began to repeat itself as Herm played a part in his eventual downfall – for, it later emerged, he was also a brandy smuggler! The disruptive quarrying days which had chipped away at the heart of Herm had gone forever.

The remains of the quarries can still be seen:

1 – Beneath the obelisk on the Common

2 – The west side of Monku

3 The first quarry on Herm behind the hotel and was originally known as La Chausee (the landing quarry)

4 – Rosière – the two biggest quarries were at Rosière. One is used today as the island rubbish dump, but rather more interesting is the fact that today it is the home of long eared owls who return here each summer to breed.

5 – Casual quarrying: boulders were picked up from the south and east coast and off loaded into barges. Some of the rocks still bear the scars of pick axes.

Mining days 1835-1838

Soon after Duncan left Herm, John Hunt, a Kent mining engineer formed the Herm Mines Company. He opened an office in the Commercial Arcade in Guernsey in 1838 where he displayed minerals and precious metals apparently mined from Sark and Herm. But he found few people prepared to invest in the venture.

Hunt sank experimental shafts seeking out silver, lead and copper in Herm and found seams containing all three. The census of 1841 records a 30 year old copper miner Robert Oliver from London living on Herm with his wife Ann and their four young children.

Hunt sank shafts in the south of the island near Rosière naming one bore hole after Mr. Gay the cheerful barman and grocer.

In 1844 more test mines were sunk in Valley Panto (they ran all the way under the garden of Le Manoir) and to the east of the island although these sites are now covered and overgrown.

Mining in Herm proved expensive and unfruitful. The mines were prone to flooding, making working conditions difficult.

The success of the silver mines in Sark offered more attractive prospects – the mining eventually fizzled out and attracted no further interest although Hunt managed to prove that a copper seam ran throughout the island which presumably still exists today.

---

*Pier in front of hotel
*Harbour
*Railway cranes and remains of railway track
*Quarries at Rosière, behind hotel, The Commons, South Coast
*Beehive prison in hotel gardens
*Hotel cottages at foot of hill
*Rosière Cottage
*Mermaid Cottages

Brandy Galore!
Old Smugglers' Tales 1867-1877

Col Fielding, a mighty builder
Compton Mackenzie

Lt Col Montague Joseph Feilden from Preston, Lancs, was the first of the island's tenants who made Herm an attractive place not just for himself – but also for visitors.

He appeared, to all intents and purposes, a highly respectable Tenant of Herm. He bought the combined lease to Herm and Jethou on September 19th, 1867 and went on to spend thousands of pounds improving the island. Feilden was responsible for opening the hotel, which was known then as The Old Inn. He extended and renovated the building, and opened a bowling saloon and billiard room.

However, he fell heavily from grace when he was discovered attempting to recoup some of his expenditure through brandy and tobacco smuggling. At one time Feilden used Jethou as a storehouse for illicit quantities of fine French brandy.

Feilden's smuggling antics presumably paid handsomely as he spent thousands of pounds modernising and renovating Herm after the devastating impact of the quarrying days.

His wealth and position as Tenant of Herm also bought him an entree to Guernsey 'society' and he enjoyed organising shooting parties for local dignitaries.

Feilden built Belvoir House, known then as Belvoir Villa, or Belle Vue, for himself and also set up a bathing hut above the beach. He built the original Rosière Steps, spent £4,500 improving the harbour (appropriately enough for a smuggler he owned four boats The Mermaid, The Hermit, The Ranger and Coquette), and modernised the outbuildings and workmen's cottages that had lain empty and derelict since the quarrying days. (His staff used large conch shells to help the boats home in the fog. One person stood on the end of Herm harbour blowing on the shell to aid the ships' return).

The White House Hotel

The White House Hotel has been open since the 1860s for passing visitors, on a bed and breakfast basis. Bartlett and Hyde were the first tenants to use the sea facing building, once used as a dining area for the quarrymen on the island, as a boarding house, but it was Feilden who took it one step further, spent money on the building and opened it up as an hotel. It was closed during the tenancy of Prince Blücher although it was reopened on a limited level by Sir Compton Mackenzie. It was the home of the next tenant, Sir Percival Perry, who named the building The White House after his American connections with the motor magnate Henry Ford. The hotel reopened after the Second World War and has been developed and extended by the present day tenants.

11 – Visitors arriving in an open topped boat around the turn of the century.

Feilden employed Henry West as his bailiff in the early days of his tenancy. West, from a small village near Stonehenge, was to become a reliable helping hand and gamekeeper on the island, working for Feilden as well as the Trappist monks, the Maxwells, and Prince Blücher, and raising a total of 13 children.

When West answered the advertisement for bailiff neither he nor his wife Sarah had ever seen the sea. The boat taking them to their new island home made them both desperately seasick, but they managed to survive and moved into one of the row of cottages overlooking the fields of Herm. Seven of their large brood were born on Herm in the late 1800s.

Feilden was the first to develop the hotel, charging bed and board for 6/- a day, and offering fresh oysters from the beds he laid down at Oyster Point.

He imported Spanish oxen, and it is thought that the unusual oxen shoeing stocks situated at the back of Forge Cottage in the Manor Village – once a blacksmith's cottage like Rosière Cottage, equipped with bellows – dates from this time. Oxen were used to pull carts carrying the boulders which Feilden used to heighten the original dry stone walls.

12 – The Fox, beached at Belvoir – the islanders were thanked for their help in salvaging her.

Only two years after buying the lease a 'secret store' of four bales of Cavendish tobacco weighing 200lbs was found by custom officials on Jethou. A clue to Feilden's secret life as a smuggler lies in his decision to employ a motley band of Bretons and Welshmen who fired warning shots if anyone dared to venture too close to Jethou, which at one point he had hoped to have joined to Herm by a giant causeway. Like other grand schemes of the past, this one also failed to materialise.

In 1873 he was fined £50 after a further cache of 50 brandy barrels was found in the two storey beach house on Jethou, and another secret store of 27 barrels of brandy on board one of his boats moored between Jethou and Herm.

Feilden denied any knowledge of the brandy. But the court found him guilty and fined him and later that year he decided to put the lease for the islands up for sale – rumours were rife that the authorities put pressure on him to go.

13 – Arriving in Herm for a day out aboard a steamer from Guernsey.

> *The description of Herm in the Gazette de Guernsey advertising the sale of the lease by Feilden in 1875 reports the island is in a 'high state of cultivation' with good pasteurage watered by fine springs.*
>
> *The Island had a newly-built farm fitted with a steam engine, workshops, hen houses, and dog kennels, and there was a daily steamer service from Guernsey and Southampton in the summer, and five days a week in the winter.*
>
> *The 'commodious hotel' was equipped with American and English bowling saloons, a billiard room and guests were offered 'first class' sporting facilities, the island being well stocked with pheasants, partridge and woodcocks.'*
>
> *The Gazette also notes the bays abound with turbot, mackerel, whiting, and mullet and the 'trade (of fishing) may be carried on with considerable profit'.*

Herm went up for sale by auction at the Mart Tokenhouse Yard in London on August 5th at 2pm – but there were no takers.

Feilden continued living on Herm, running the farm and hotel until 1877 when an entrepreneur James Considine from London bought the lease privately for £7,600. Feilden left the Channel Islands, and headed for South Africa, where, it is said, he died penniless.

Following Feilden's smuggling convictions the States of Guernsey decided it was unwise to allow future tenants to hold the lease of both islands. This clause remained in force until 1920 when both islands were leased to Sir Compton Mackenzie.

Other short term tenants

James Considine, an Irishman, held Herm for a little over a year as an investment before selling it on to Arthur Maxwell from Darlington for a small profit of £360.

Maxwell and his brother lived a raucous life on Herm for the next two years, reviving the brewery set up in Duncan's day, and using Feilden's bowling saloon for cock fighting sessions.

The pair reputedly kept a large number of dogs and Arthur Maxwell apparently enjoyed driving a dog cart at full speed down the hill to the harbour with '80 dogs in full cry' behind him, pulling up at the edge of the harbour just in time to avoid plunging into the sea! If one of his dogs disobeyed an order it was promptly shot.

The Maxwells were not quite as refined as some of the previous tenants and unable to 'fulfil the conditions of the lease' which allowed Considine to take over again.

Monks return

In 1881 Considine sub let the island to a small band of Trappist Monks from Chartres led by an Irish prior William Bourke, aged 42, who took up residence at The Manor. The monks came from France, Belgium and Luxembourg, but left after a few short months 'not having found the climate and surroundings suitable for a permanent settlement.'

The following year a second batch of Chartreuse monks from Grenoble paid Considine £6,800 for the Herm lease. They stayed only 18 months in Herm en route to a new monastery in Sussex, although during this short spell apparently planted eucalyptus trees on the island.

By 1884 the island lease was up for auction again in London and although there were once more no immediate takers, James Linklater from Leith, Scotland, eventually paid £7,500 for the lease.

He had plans to set up a major fishing industry from Herm, operating 280 fishing boats, and a salting and processing plant on the island. None of these elaborate plans saw the light of day and by 1889 events were in place for the creation of an entirely new use for Herm – a private kingdom.

During Linklater's tenancy about 40 people lived on Herm. One day a steamer, The Fox, en route from Stockton to Guernsey carrying iron pipes and coal, struck a rock in the Little Russell and was beached on Belvoir Bay.

The residents helped salvage the load and a few days later were invited to a 'thank you' supper at the hotel organised to 'repay the kindness of the inhabitants.'

---

* Belvoir House

*Rosière Steps

*Old oyster beds at Oyster Point

*White House Hotel, known as the Old Inn

*Improvements to the harbour

*Oxen shoeing stocks

*Some of the old photographs which appear in this book date from the time the Trappist Monks were in residence on Herm.

An island kingdom
1889-1915

"Halfway up the road a meadow ascends between coppices of blackthorn to the top of the world and beyond that to a grove of pines planted by my predecessor Prince Blücher von Wahlstatt"
— **Sir Compton Mackenzie, Herm and its Secrets, 1932.**

The story of the 26 year tenancy of Herm by the Blücher family begins happily enough, but rather like the best fairy stories which feature princes and princesses, woods, castles and curses, there is also a 'powerful giant' – in this case the combined weight of the British Crown and the Guernsey authorities.

After a long and mostly happy tenancy Prince Gebhard Lebrecht Blücher von Wahlstatt 3rd, grandson of the famous Prussian Field Marshal Gebhard Blücher who fought with Wellington at Waterloo, faced the humiliation of being evicted from the island and branded an 'enemy alien' at the outbreak of the First World War.

Despite the fact that the Prince had renounced his nationality he was evicted from Herm along with his third, much younger, wife. His son, daughter in law, and grandchild, all members of the Prussian aristocracy by birth were also told to leave their island home, as they were considered 'undesirable' residents of Crown owned property in view of the looming Great War.

The fact that the Prince was on record opposing the course of German politics and that he was effectively 'stateless' held no weight with the British Government, embarrassed by having a famous,'well connected' Prussian living on Crown property.

Prince Blücher never got over the loss of his fondly held island home, and went to Germany where he died in July 1916, just a few months after leaving Herm. He was a heartbroken man of 80.

The Prince arrives in Herm

Prince Blücher first heard about Herm through his bank, The West Bank of Silesia, which bought the lease from Linklater for £7,000 in 1889, after a year of overtures. The Crown authorities were later to look into the link between the bank and Prince Blücher and came to the conclusion that 'in reality it represents some private financial arrangement of the Blücher family'.

The sale to the wealthy Prussians took a year to complete, and caused quite a stir in the local papers of the time and some fear was expressed in Whitehall that Herm might pass into the hands of a foreign Government. Locally, gossip and rumour were rife over the proposed plans for the island.

Local folk need not have worried unduly, for by 1890, the 54 year old hereditary Prince was installed on the island and had begun to transform Herm into his own private kingdom well away from the claustrophobic Prussian court life he had begun to detest. Many of the improvements and changes to the island still exist today.

Prince Blücher was an extremely wealthy man with an hereditary fortune of around £500,000, and annual income of some £80,000 from his numerous estates which had passed down through the family from his famous grandfather.

He already owned two castles, one in Rodun, (now part of the Czech republic) and another in Krieblowitz (now Southern Poland) where the coach which had carried the defeated Napoleon was once housed, as well as a palace in Berlin and estates elsewhere abroad.

But he had been looking for a chance to make a fresh start. And Herm Island seemed the ideal opportunity.

The Prince had been involved in a long and drawn out court case with the City of Berlin – which he lost. According to a newspaper article of the time this situation

14 – Prince Blücher

'appears to have confirmed in him his hatred of Prussia and all connected with it.'

On a brighter note he had just married a much younger wife, the Countess Elizabeth von Perponder-Sedlnitzky who, at the time of their move to Herm was 32 years old (22 years younger than the Prince) and expecting her first and only child. Until this second marriage he had been a widower for 20 years.

The Prince already had five children by his first marriage who were all grown up.

Relations with at least two of his elder sons were strained to say the least; they were both disinherited and there were numerous rows over allowances and money and the fact they wanted to join the Prussian Army, a move he resented because of his feelings of bitterness towards his native homeland.

Herm provided the perfect escape route for the newly weds and the Prince set about creating his own personal haven amid the tranquillity and seclusion of the Channel Islands.

Like others before him, and countless others since, he fell in love with the peaceful serenity of the island.

Prince Blücher transformed Herm by :

* turning the traditional farmhouse into "Herm Castle" by installing granite crenelated keeps and squaring off the roof of the house, and the buildings connected to it and establishing 26 apartments and offices.

* transforming the 18th century mill at the back of the Manor into a watch tower, with matching crenelated surround.

* using Belvoir House as a 'summer retreat' and installing well stocked gardens and a freshwater pond.

* restoring St. Tugual's chapel – rescuing it from its former use as a laundry.

* installing granite pillars and a gate at the foot of The Drive

* building a winter garden in the grounds of The Manor

* creating walled gardens planted with soft fruit trees and vineries

* building the archway at Rosière Steps to create the illusion of an 'entrance' to the island.

46

* planting many trees, namely the distinctive Monterey pines and many exotic plants up the sweeping drive and in the back of The Manor.
* stocking the island as a game reserve, bringing in pheasants, roe deer, emus, and somewhat eccentrically 30 wallabies. The Prince had plans to introduce lions to the Rosière quarry, although (perhaps fortunately) this plan never materialised.

The Prince imported servants and finely dressed footmen from his native land and filled his home with antique furniture and paintings.

On October 10th 1890 Princess Elizabeth Blücher gave birth to the Prince's most beloved and favoured son Count Lothair Blücher in "Herm Castle", today's Manor house.

According to papers lodged in the Island Archives Office in Guernsey Prince Blücher transferred the island 'bond' valued at £7,000 (this was the amount paid for the lease) over to his baby son's name in September of 1891, as well £2,000 that had been advanced by the bank for building and repairs on the island. He later named the Count as the chief inheritor of his estates.

Effectively the Prince signed over Herm to his son although he remained in charge and control of the island.

15. The newly completed Herm Castle and surrounding 'village.'

Presumably the Prince hoped that by entering into this arrangement for his son it would mean he would have a safe haven whatever happened to his estates in Prussia (the family were later to lose them all to the Communists). But the Prince was to be proved wrong.

His second marriage to Elizabeth ended sadly when she died in March 1894 at the Prince's castle home in Prussia – her son Count Lothair was just four years old, and he was brought up and educated in Herm with private tutors, and later in England. The Prince remained a widower for the next 11 years when he decided to marry again.

The Blücher family tell of his passion for Princess Katerina Radziwell, a notorious writer and journalist who wrote 'soap operas' of the day about Berlin court life. She was the mother of three daughters, and Prince Blücher made it known that he would like to marry one of them.

The family story that endures tells of the the three young girls being approached in their schoolroom by their father who told them "Prince Blücher has offered to marry one of you". It was the youngest, Princess Wanda, who saw the perfect opportunity to marry an older, wealthy man, and to escape from the overbearing shadow of her mother and strike out into the world and into society.

16. The White House, when it was Count Blücher's home.---

And so on May 6th, 1905, in St. Petersburg, Princess Wanda Radziwell, barely out of her teens, married Prince Blücher who was then aged 69. Ironically this oddly arranged marriage threw together the Prince's son, Count Lothair (16 at the time) and his future wife Princess Louise "Lulu" Radziwell (Princess Wanda's eldest sister) which in time was to prove a great love match.

Despite the Prince's age, the couple went on to have three children, a son and two daughters, while they lived in Herm bringing Prince Blücher's total number of offspring to nine.

A rich lifestyle

Prince Blücher kept his steamer The White Heather moored in the harbour using it to attend church in Guernsey on Sundays. A carriage pulled by white horses would meet the family at the harbour and carry them to Mass. Occasionally Sunday services were held at Rosière Cottage. He also used the 17 ton cutter The Mermaid which travelled to Guernsey once a week to collect groceries for the 10 families living on Herm at the time.

> *Prince Blücher entertained British royalty during his tenancy. Princess Alice, the Countess of Athlone, visited Herm as a girl. The island visit was arranged during a trip to Guernsey aboard the Royal Yacht. A carriage was sent ahead to carry her about Herm and many years she later recalled in conversation "picking up shells, tiny cowries on a beautiful beach" and meeting Prince Blücher.*

Although vastly wealthy the Prince was guarded with his money and seemed to enjoy court room battles. The Prince and Princess Wanda, were involved in a lengthy court case over the non payment of £200 for a christening layette for their baby born in Herm in 1906, a year after their wedding.

The couple claimed that the Princess's mother, the outspoken Princess Katerina Radziwell, had promised to pay and the garments had been ordered on her behalf.

Princess Radziwell denied this and claimed that the Prince could easily afford to pay 'as he had an income of £80,000 a year.'

The apparently petty dispute was finally resolved in favour of the Prince and Princess, and against Princess Radziwell who was ordered to pay the debt.

Meanwhile the couple enjoyed their life on Herm. The wallabies were a great talking point locally. The animals were allowed to roam over the island quite freely, and would sleep around Belvoir or Valley Panto depending on the direction of the wind. Late at night they could be heard scampering up The Drive.

Unfortunately 27 of the poor creatures were shot by the Prince's cook and butler, despite the men being expressly forbidden to shoot on the island. The case went to court, and the men who apologised in a letter to Prince Blücher, and burst into tears in the courtroom, were nonetheless sentenced to a month's hard labour for their misdeed.

Heavenly retreat

Princess Wanda was charmed by Herm, and fell in love with Belvoir Bay in particular which she used as her own exclusive retreat, away from her elderly husband and barring even the uniformed servants from treading the golden sand.

17 – Island children at The Harbour in the late 1800s.

Prince Blücher, appreciating the local interest in the island, allowed visitors access to Herm once a week. For a toll of 6d visitors were permitted to walk from the harbour to Shell Beach – but only on Mondays. Stern notices were put up along the pathway warning trespassers not to leave the path or roam over the island.

Meanwhile Blücher's son Count Lothair, was growing up to be a fine young man.

His father had renounced his nationality and was technically 'stateless' which allowed the Count to choose his new nationality. He chose to become British.

The descendants of the Blüchers of Herm describe Count Lothair as 'truly the golden boy of the family'. As a young man he joined the Royal Guernsey Militia as an officer and cut a fine, dashing figure, appearing at local social gatherings particularly boating regattas.

Meanwhile his relationship with Princess Lulu Radziwell, the older sister of Princess Wanda blossomed on Herm during visits to her sister at Herm Castle. He eventually married the Princess, who was a good 10 years older than her husband, when he was barely 20.

The Count and Countess moved into the White House and spent a vast amount of money renovating and improving the former hotel. Gardens blossomed around the house which had a large entrance hall, fireplace and staircase, five bedrooms and two bathrooms, a separate servants hall and quarters and gun room.

The Countess Lulu, like her sister, chose her own private walkway in the grounds of the White House, barring the servants from the area so nothing could disturb the unparalleled views of the west coast of the island and across to Guernsey. (This walkway has now been reopened and is available for use by hotel guests).

Despite the unusual family set up, the four got on well and Prince Blücher developed a more loving rapport with his son than with any of his other grown children.

Count Lothair, as a young man, often represented his father, meeting visitors and members of excursions organised by La Société Guernesiaise and was considered courteous and kindly.

Between them the two families employed 30 staff, some of whom worked on a small farm providing fresh milk, eggs, vegetables and fruit.

Storm clouds gather

All was well on Herm (the Count and Countess had started a family) until the storm clouds gathered with the lead up to and eventual outbreak of the First World War.

Although the two families were considered to be good and generous employers, and excellent tenants of the island, the British and Guernsey authorities decided that because of the Prince's Prussian birth there could be no other course of action other than to classify the whole Blücher family as 'enemy aliens'.

The Prince was interned on Guernsey but he soon left and went to Germany where he died the following year never fully recovering from the loss of the island.

The Blücher tenancy was the subject of lengthy debates by the States of Guernsey and HM Treasury in London who also referred the matter to the Foreign Office. At one stage officials feared that if the Blüchers were ousted reprisals may be taken against British held property in Germany. Nevertheless it was agreed that the family had to go. The only way to remove them was a change in the law which would allow the Guernsey authorities to evict the family.

18 – The wallabies introduced to Herm by Prince Blücher.

The 'fee farm lease' arrangement set up since the 1700s was cancelled by a Projet de Loi (a special change in the law) passed in the autumn of 1915.

The Count's Fury

On October 6th 1915 HM's Receiver General in Guernsey wrote to Count Blücher ordering him to make all the necessary preparations to leave the island and giving him just a fortnight's notice.

The speed at which the decision was eventually taken infuriated the Count. He made the necessary arrangements for his wife, who was expecting their second child, to leave Herm and move to Guernsey but he wrote back an angry letter to HM Receivers Office in Guernsey stating:

"I wish to point out that this island has been my home for a number of years and that I have a very large amount of furniture and other valuable possessions here including livestock, horses and poultry.

"It is a matter of absolute impossibility to dispose of or remove these possessions in so short a time with the labour and transport accommodation at my disposal and under the present unfavourable weather conditions. It is hardly necessary to point out that this is causing me very grave expense. To remove all my belongings would probably take three or four months perhaps longer ......"

After this appeal, he was granted a further two months to remove his possessions from the island.

Meanwhile the two sisters, Princess Wanda and the Countess Louise, were both very sad, if not distraught, at the outcome of events.

When Princess Wanda found herself in the humiliating position of being told to leave the island and to return to her warring homeland, she laid a curse upon the next tenant of the island – wishing him misfortune. (The next tenant turned out to be the novelist Sir Compton Mackenzie, who took the curse seriously and believed in its effectiveness – see page 61). She returned to Prussia but her sister the Countess Lulu stayed on and after their eviction from Herm the couple moved into a house called Elmwood in the Catel district and then later moved to Havilland Hall.

There was support for them locally and when Count Blücher received the notice to quit, an editorial appeared in the local paper supporting him, pointing out that island staff would lose their homes and jobs as a result of the move.

Later the staff unanimously passed a motion expressing sympathy with Count Blücher and 'regret at losing an ideal employer'.

The Crown authorities took no notice of the feelings of local people and no heed of the Blücher's personal losses.

In a letter appealing to a family nanny to come and work for them Countess "Lulu" wrote revealingly: *"You know that the Government took away our island which of course belonged to the Prince and not to my husband. But in reality we are much harder hit than my father in law because we built and furnished the house we lived in and greatly improved the island with our own money and intended to make it our permanent home. Now we have had to leave our house without the slightest compensation which I think most unjust ......This has hit us terribly hard for my husband can get no money from Germany and my own Prussian money is much diminished by the bad exchange."*

19· The White Heather, the Blücher family's private steamer.

War Years

Herm was effectively shut down the following year although a small military garrison was posted on the island. There was a detachment of the South Staffordshire Regiment which was sent to Herm as a precaution against German submarines landing spies. Herbert Hughes, who later became famous as a composer, was the subaltern in charge.

On Easter Monday, April 24th, 1916 the Guernsey Steam Towing and Trading Company, were refused permission to take a party of visitors to the island because 'the Island of Herm would be closed as from April 8th to all civilians under any circumstances.'

However, in 1917 E.H. Weadon and sons, both growers of La Couture, Guernsey, offered £100 to rent Herm's farm land with buildings and cottages'. The Company grew potatoes on the island despite the rampaging rabbit population. A plan to set up a German PoW camp on the island was rejected.

20 – There was restricted access but local people could still come on certain days to visit the island.

Count Attempts to Regain Herm

After the war Count Blücher made a final attempt at leasing back Herm with a collective of other Guernsey businessmen, but his application was flatly refused.

In a letter to the Receiver General in Guernsey he suggested that *'some friends of mine Englishmen and Guernsey men, I may mention'* had been prepared to form a syndicate to buy the lease of Herm for 50 years.

The proposal, he said, would be to develop the island *'into a sound farming and growing proposition and secondly to attract visitors'*.

With some foresight he adds: *'My friends and I have no doubt but that this scheme could prove a sound commercial undertaking and lead to the establishment of a permanent and prosperous colony in Herm'*.

In the same letter he suggested that he would be seeking compensation of some £15,000 for the money spent on the island if he was unable to return to Herm to live.

The Count's idea for a syndicate fell on deaf ears; his appeal to return to his island home and his request for compensation refused. A year later Princess Wanda, now a widow, started proceedings to claim £9,000 compensation for the loss of Herm on behalf of the Count. There is no record of any compensation ever being paid.

Count Blücher died only a decade later in his 30s, of tuberculosis in Switzerland.

Blücher links live on

There is still a Blücher link in Guernsey. One remaining relative, Countess Lydia Blücher, a great granddaughter of the Prince, has a home in the island.

New era dawns

After the dark years of the war could there be a chance of a happier, brighter future for Herm?

Just around the corner was the start of an entirely new era and one which echoes still down the years – for in the ensuing years Herm charmed two important novelists, and it was during the post war years that Herm played an important inspirational part in the creation of a number of literary works.

Belvoir Bay and Shell Beach

Rural Herm

The Manor House

Oxen shoeing stocks

Rosière Steps and Rosière Cottage

Fisherman's Cottage

The Seahorse, Herm's own cargo vessel

The story of Count Lothair and Countess Lulu Blücher's meeting and marriage is still seen by the family as one of the greatest love stories in the Blücher family history.

Countess Lydia Blücher, a great granddaughter of Prince Blücher, who in 1995 still had a home in Guernsey, says: "It was a good match, they loved each other very much, although he was younger than she was.

"Lulu was considered in the family to be a warm hearted person with a most generous spirit, and it was a great loss when the Count died in his early 30s of TB."

"The marriage of the Prince, his father and the Princess Wanda, was not so much of a romance. But the Prince proved to be a very energetic man, with children of all generations. He had a good charisma, and certainly more than a touch of eccentricity. I would describe him as like one of today's wheeler dealers prepared to take people to court and more than a bit quarrelsome!"

21 – The Mermaid – a cargo vessel carrying groceries for the 10 families of Herm.

*The crenelated keep at Le Manoir

*The Archway at Rosière Steps designed to create the effect of an entrance to the island

*The Round Tower (formerly the Old Mill built in the late 1700s and transformed into a watchtower by Prince Blücher)

*Walled gardens in the Manor Village

* Stone pillars at the foot of The Drive which featured large wrought iron gates to keep the visitors 'at bay'

*Monterey Pines – still a feature of the Herm horizon, eucalyptus trees in Belvoir Valley and The Drive area

*The Deer Park, where Prince Blücher based the wallabies

Literary and Artistic Connections

" ......whatever one might write or say about an island like Herm, of its romantic history, of the pirates hanged there in chains, of the treasure found and the skeletons dug up, of the Neolithic monuments, of the monks, wreckers, and quarrymen and smugglers who have lived there, of the trippers who twice a week in summer cross from Trinidad to Tobago for their cannibal feasts on the Shell Beach, leaving more than one footprint to horrify us Crusoes when they have departed– whatever one might say, the island will keep its secret."
Sir Compton Mackenzie, My Life and Times.

Herm has been the inspiration for countless articles, at least four novels, a children's fairy story and a book of poems, and two autobiographies. The constantly moving and changing sea around the island also inspired Tim Thompson who is considered to be one of the foremost marine artists in the world today and who lived in Herm during his childhood in the 1950s.

The island captured the imagination of some of the "Bloomsbury set" in the 1930s as well as D.H. Lawrence, the most controversial and evocative writer of his time who wrote descriptively about the island although he never actually visited Herm.

But it was Sir Compton Mackenzie, the novelist, who was the first writer to put Herm on the map when he fell for the island's natural charms.

Mackenzie comes to Herm

After the war, and the sad end to the Blücher tenancy, the Receiver General's Office in Guernsey, representatives of the Crown officials in London, agreed that efforts should be made to relet the island. An advertisement was placed in The Times inviting applications for the 60 year lease of Herm for £900 a year and of Jethou for £100 a year.

The advertisement was spotted by Mackenzie's agent Martin Secker who promptly showed it to the novelist sensing it would appeal to his love of islands. But there was also a hidden agenda.

At the time of the advertisement Mackenzie was moving ahead with plans to set sail to the South Seas with his friend D.H. Lawrence as an answer to 'the complication of life in post war Europe'. The pair even planned to colonise some little known islands off the coast of New Zealand.

Secker was opposed to the idea, fearing he would have to work hard obtaining commissions for Mackenzie's work as a result of the travels.

> *Mackenzie, a self-confessed 'island addict' originally advertised for a companion for his South Seas journey stating "novelist requires for long voyage expert shorthand typist, healthy, young, good sailor not afraid of luggage or savages."*
>
> *He received 57 replies, but when he and DH Lawrence met up in Capri where Mackenzie had a home, they talked over the plan and it was agreed they should go together.*

Mackenzie had gone as far as inspecting a 134 ton ketch up for sale at 7,500 guineas equipped with 'large salon, four cabins and a smoking lounge'.

He wrote excitedly to Lawrence about the vessel, called The Lavengro, and in July and August Mackenzie made strenuous efforts to raise the money for the boat.

When Secker showed him a copy of The Times inviting applications for the "60 year lease of Herm" it had the instant, desired effect.

Mackenzie later wrote: *"A ketch can always be obtained; desirable islands are rare. I had long ago marked down Herm as a desirable island, the possessor of which might compete one day with Tresco, and Tresco has the finest garden in Europe.*

One of the characteristics of island lovers is an ability to make up the mind quickly and to change it as rapidly. The voyage was postponed; the island was acquired."

The decision to abandon the South Seas plan angered Lawrence. He initially hid his feelings and in October 1919 Lawrence wrote to Mackenzie *"I have been hearing about the islands, Herm and the one ending in "hou": They sound rather fascinating. Are you going to farm Herm? – and who is going to be your farmer? I've half a mind to come and help in the stormy Channel."*

The first sign that Lawrence was indeed furious at being 'dumped' by his friend in favour of two islands came in another letter in which he wrote: *"What is this I hear about the Channel Isles? the Lord of the Isles. I shall write a skit on you one day."*

Their relationship deteriorated several years later when Lawrence did indeed write a 'skit', a short story entitled The Man Who Loved Islands, which Mackenzie saw as an account of his tenancy of Herm and Jethou. (See page 68)

The magic of Herm

Mackenzie was accepted by the Crown authorities as a suitable tenant and several decades later he wrote in Octave Five of his autobiography "My Life and Times": *"I can feel the magic of Herm still when I remember the time I stepped out of the Watch Me, the island boat, with her bearded skipper and walked up the steps to set foot for the first time upon the little granite pier."*

Although his island addiction had led him to Herm, Mackenzie soon discovered that running the island was expensive and difficult.

He complained about the fact over dinner with Count Lothair Blücher who was living in Guernsey.

One evening the Countess told Mackenzie she was worried about him on Herm because her youngest sister, Princess Wanda had 'prayed to the island spirits to bring misfortune to the next tenant'. The Countess told Mackenzie about the curse, she said, because she did not think he was the sort of person that her sister would have wished bad luck.

Mackenzie blamed the Princess's wish for misfortune when he lost a film contract worth £3,500 within a month of taking on Herm. And it was remembered after an unnerving experience on Herm two years later. (See page 63).

Meanwhile, Mackenzie chose a cottage next to The Manor as his home. (It could have been the present day Lady Perry's House as he describes it as being linked by a covered walkway – at that time an orangery linked the back of The Manor where a ballroom, a legacy of Blücher's era, once stood, to the cottage. When Major Wood took over the tenancy in 1949 he found a number of old gramophone records which may have belonged to Mackenzie in this cottage).

61

He would not feel at home at The Manor, he wrote, as he considered it to be "the ugliest building in Europe", nor at the Count's former home, the present day White House Hotel, which he thought too close to the sea for the good of his sciatica.

He writes with painful honesty: *"About a week after I had established myself on Herm I wrote to tell Martin Secker that I thought I had made a mistake."* Nevertheless he was prepared to give it a go and got on with creating the island of his dreams. He envisaged the island becoming a gardeners' and farmers' paradise. Later he was to write that the first full year of his tenancy was one of the most enjoyable years of his life despite his growing money troubles.

He set about restoring the neglected island, cutting back bracken 'five foot high', burning bramble thickets, and waging war on the rabbits. He put his writing on hold for six months as he tackled the day to day problems of the island.

He had a great love of plants and gardening, and employed gardener Basil Leng, (writing to the Glasnevin Botanical gardens in Dublin for a recommendation). Some of the plants he introduced to the island still flourish such as New Zealand flax, Royal Fern, and a prolific Fuchsia bush.

One of the first problems was the drought summer of 1921 when the sun shone constantly between March and October. The water supply on the island became low and crops suffered.

The summer also brought out the day visitors to Herm who he considered a 'great trial'. They were allowed on the island twice a week for a toll of 6d and could walk to Shell Beach, although they inevitably found their way around to Belvoir Bay.

Mackenzie complained that they 'wandered all over the island' and was amused by one occasion when Hamlet returned from Belvoir with some women's underwear snatched from the beach!

He wrote: *"Most people ask me what I do with myself on Herm. Island lovers ask how I find time to do my own work; I hardly need say that the island lovers understand the real difficulties of life there, I write at night and even then on moonlit nights I grudge the time. I could easily amuse myself for ever watching birds."*

62

He was finding it difficult with financial burdens and Herm's constant need for full time attention.

To raise his spirits Mackenzie bought a gramophone, and it was to prove to be his next "great passion" triggering the launch of The Gramophone Magazine which he wrote and edited from Herm and later from Jethou. By the spring of 1922 he had a collection of some 200 records.

One of the oddest sights must have been Mackenzie driving his mother round the island in a Victorian chaise driven by one of his horses imported from Guernsey.

It was his mother who suggested that Mackenzie develop the island for tourism although he was, initially, quite against the idea considered:

"Decent people were turned into savages by the mere fact of having paid sixpence to land on the island."

Nevertheless he pressed ahead with plans to open up the hotel which had previously been known as the Old Inn (the present day White House) and name it The Mermaid Tavern (sic), and commissioned a boat with which to develop the tourist trade the following year. In the summer of 1922 he had secured a licence for the hotel and the first major function of the 'tourist season' during Mackenzie's tenancy was held in 1922 – an al fresco lunch for the directors of the Great Western Railway.

Maybe he felt he was 'selling out' to the visitors, for it was soon after this event that Mackenzie felt the 'elemental spirits' of the island come alive. He wrote of the experience: *"It was soon after that visit by the Great Western board of directors that towards dusk I walked along to the Common and as I reached the dolmens was seized suddenly with a panic. "It is hopeless to even try to convey that peculiar feeling of terror which the Greeks recognised and which the Psalms of David recognised. I hurried, half running, back to my cottage. I recalled what Countess Blücher had told me about the prayer her sister had uttered to the spirits of the island that the next tenant should be unfortunate."*

"Next morning I went back to where I had been seized by the panic and prayed to the spirits of the island.

"I wound up by telling them if they wanted somebody on whom they could vent their ill will more appropriately than on me they should choose a profiteer of war."

Mackenzie found it difficult to believe it was 'mere coincidence' that a Guernsey businessman should invite Sir Percival Perry to visit Herm for lunch – the very next day.

Just a year later Perry, who made a fortune out of disposing of old war vehicles and later became the chairman of the Ford Motor Company in the UK became the next Tenant of Herm.

In his autobiography Mackenzie reveals a jaded opinion of Sir Percival Perry, who became Lord Perry of Stock Harvard in 1938. His views must have been influenced by the time consuming negotiations they became involved in during the handover of the lease. Mackenzie wanted to sell the lease for £10,000, the amount he had spent on the island but the pair settled on £7,500.

Mackenzie left Herm, never to return, to live on the neighbouring island of Jethou, which he felt had a far more benign air and where he discovered the smaller more manageable size of the island suited him better. He spent eight happy years on Jethou and he never returned to Herm although every day he was able to see the golden shores just a short distance away. Like others before him he had loved, and lost Herm.

"I have never put foot on Herm since I walked down the Rosière Steps and embarked on a small boat to be rowed across the Percee to Jethou on that tranquil summer morning. As I write these words over 40 years later I can still hear my footsteps crunching on the beach of that dearly loved little island."

During his tenancy of Herm, Sir Compton Mackenzie had the following works published:

The Altar Steps (Cassell, 1932), The Seven Ages of Woman (Secker, 1923); The Old Men of the Sea (Cassell, 1924) later published as Paradise for Sale; Vol One of The Gramophone Magazine, April 1923; Gramophone Nights (Heinneman, 1923) Santa Claus in Summer (Constable, 1924).

Mackenzie also made a start on the book Buttercups and Daisies which was eventually published by Cassell in 1925.

He also wrote many articles about his life on Herm for different publications including the Countryman and the Daily Telegraph. Mackenzie wrote a further 14 books during his eight years on Jethou.

Sir Compton Mackenzie introduced several plants to Herm during his three years as Tenant. A Royal Fern situated near the toilets between Shell Beach and Belvoir Bay still flourishes despite a vigorous Fuchsia which grows nearby which was also planted for Mackenzie.

Another interesting plant from Mackenzie's time on Herm is the Belladonna Lily *(Amaryllis belladonna)* planted on the south side of The Drive above the harbour which flowers in the autumn.

Literary Inspiration

Fairy Gold by Sir Compton Mackenzie

Based on Herm and Jethou, the novel is light-hearted, romantic and full of colourful prose.

It is worth reading for the descriptions of Herm alone, which rise off the page as strong and true today as they did in the 1930s. Indeed, part of the fun of the book is pinpointing parts of Herm from the descriptions.

It is quite clear the islands and Mackenzie's own feelings for them, and his experiences in dealing with Sir Percival Perry in the handover of the lease were the inspiration for the book.

Oddly, the island is given an east–west reversal, so that Belvoir, known in the book as Greenwater Cove is on the west coast, and The Drive slopes down to the left rather than to the right.

22 – Sir Compton Mackenzie on Herm with Rosière Steps in the background, dictating to his assistant James Eastwood, a journalist.

The Neolithic remains on The Common are given far greater prominence, restored with literary licence, to what might have been their original size.

Mackenzie lyrically describes parts of the island, recognisable today. Of Greenwater Cove (Belvoir) he writes *"......it possessed all anybody could imagine that a small cove in a small island ought to possess.*

"It was reached from the top of Roon (Herm) by a grassy valley that dived down out of what was at first glance a perfectly ordinary field which no one would have suspected of being on the frontiers of fairyland."

"The beach, which had the texture and colour of finely ground macaroons appeared at superficial glance to be formed of dry sand; but a closer inspection of this bright crescent shared by green land and green sea revealed that it was composed entirely of shells. They were every shape and hue and degree of perfection – minute caps of liberty, wrought from alabaster lace, fairy horns of ivory rose dyed, where they had touched the lips of their tiny trumpeters, large scallops piebald and iron grey, infinitesimal fans that flamed against the light with elfin sunsets, and white cups that held in their hollows the flush of elfin dawns; sea mussels dipped in damson juice and wine; limpets spotted like pards; diminutive conches carmine-tipped; winkles of orange and citron; winkles of primrose and amber; winkles of cream and fawn of chestnut, cinnamon, and rich mahogany; lavender winkles lilac slashed and diced with pearl."

And of The Common:

"Their footsteps crackled on the prickly dead stems of the burnet roses that here and there in thick mats bronzed the turf, crackled too on the tiny bones and skulls of rabbits and on snail shells wind dried to a diaphanous lightness, then for a while moved silently over banks of golden green moss more vivid than any carpet of Samarcand."

There is a supernatural element in Fairy Gold, reflecting Mackenzie's own strongly held beliefs about mystical powers at work on Herm.

In the story a garrison of soldiers are based on the island of Roon (Herm). The central character, Dick Deverell, in charge of the garrison falls in love with Vivien Romare, daughter of the island's owner, Sir Morgan Romare.

When a new Captain takes over and plans to dig trenches in the area of Neolithic remains on the island he is appalled at this 'vandalism' and Sir Morgan's daughter Vivien is also upset. "You will all be cursed by what you have done," she says. Soon afterwards her beloved brother Mungo is killed, and her father risks losing Roon because of money troubles.

Sir Morgan discovers 'fairy gold' beneath a neolithic cromlech, real Bronze Age gold.

Soon another character Sir Caleb Fuller, appears on the scene. Modelled, it is suggested, on Sir Percival Perry he attempts to take over the island and has plans to open it up to tourists.

Rather like Perry did in real life, Sir Caleb Fuller wanted to tidy and paint the island and build a golf course.

Deverell and Vivien hatch a plan to save the island – which eventually succeeds even though Vivien's father says of the island *"It will never pay as a farm. It will never pay as a quarry. Copper and silver mining were a failure. What other way is there of making money out of it? …*

"By developing it, … By developing it as a pleasure resort."

Roon escapes the attentions of the entrepreneur and is allowed to become a private family estate once more as the spirits of the island are pacified.

The Man Who Loved Islands by DH Lawrence

This short story explores the theme of isolation through the experiences of a man who takes possession of three small islands, two situated close together modelled on Herm and Jethou and a third 'to the north' of the country. (When Mackenzie left Jethou he moved to a Scottish isle.) Mackenzie considered the story to be an offensive attack on his life and times in Herm and Jethou. Mackenzie's wife, Faith Mackenzie, also a writer, described the story as *"a malicious caricature, a monstrous perversion of the facts".*

She was undoubtedly cross as much with herself as anyone for she had unwittingly given Lawrence the ammunition to write the story by describing Herm to him over suppers in the warm Mediterranean atmosphere of Capri where Lawrence returned to live in 1926.

Although she spent time on Herm, Faith was not as passionate about the place as her husband, and she considered that he was turning his back on their cosmopolitan way of life 'to bury himself on an expensive rock in the English Channel.'

DH Lawrence writes of Herm –

"It was quite near home, no palm trees nor boom of surf on the reef, nor any of that kind of thing but a good solid dwelling house, rather gloomy, above the landing place and beyond a small farmhouse with sheds and a few outlying fields. Down on the little landing bay were three cottages in a row, like coastguards' cottages, all neat and whitewashed.

What could be more cosy and home like? It was four miles if you walked all round your island through the gorse and blackthorn bushes above the steep rocks of the sea and down in little glades where the primroses grew.

If you walked straight over the two humps of hills, the length of it, through the rocky fields where the cows lay chewing, and through the rather sparse oats, on into the gorse again, and so to the cliffs' edge, it took you only twenty minutes.

And when you came to the edge you could see another, bigger island lying beyond, and as you returned over the turf where the short, downland cowslips nodded, you saw to the east still another island, a tiny one this time, like the calf of a cow. This tiny island also belonged to the islander."

And he accurately describes the powerful natural attractions of the island:

"little glades where the primroses grew … a snow of blackthorn with blackbirds calling out of the whiteness … blue apparition of hyacinths … wild roses faintly fragrant through the haze … fields of hay … foxgloves … marsh marigolds blazing … scent of honeysuckle …"

Mackenzie was irritated at the characterisation of the islander. (But remember, Mackenzie used the same ploy himself in Fairy Gold, when he devised the unflattering character of Sir Caleb Fuller, thinly disguised as Sir Percival Perry!)

The islander is portrayed as a man who increasingly becomes isolated, bitter, eventually beginning to lose a grip on life. *"There is a danger of becoming an islander"*, Lawrence writes.

Lawrence's fictional islander, like Mackenzie, experiences 'mystical feelings' *"strange awarenesses of old, far gone men and other influences; men of Gaul with big moustaches who had been on his island and had vanished from the face of it, but not out of the air of night.*

They were still there, hurtling their big violent, unseen bodies through the night. And there were priests, with golden knives and mistletoe; then other priests with a crucifix; then pirates with murder on the sea."

Mackenzie's tenancy was undoubtedly the starting point of the story, according to David Shayter, a lecturer in English at Gwent College of Education, who has made a study of this literary relationship and the involvement of Herm.

"There was sufficient cruelty in the portrayal to suggest that Lawrence was out for Mackenzie's blood". The reference to the island having 'no palm trees' and being 'close to home' was seen as a cutting reference to the fact Herm was not a South Seas island.

Mackenzie threatened to sue two publishers who wanted the story – Secker and Heinneman – and as a result Lawrence failed to get an advance payment for the work. Mackenzie only let the matter go after Lawrence's death in 1930 and the story was eventually published in 1933 in The Lovely Lady Collection. It is still a delightful and highly evocative read.

(Quotations from "The Man who Loved Islands" printed with the permission of the estate of Frieda Lawrence Ravagli.)

23 – The gates were in place at the bottom of The Drive to keep the 'savages' out!

71

The Island of Enchantment by Percival and Catherine Perry

"And so the fairies arrived, and from that day Hame has been called the Island of Enchantment by all who love it"

Sir Percival Perry and his wife Lady Catherine Perry, were enchanted by the island from the moment they set eyes upon it. Such passionate feelings about Herm are common amongst visitors and residents alike who either feel an instant 'pull' towards the island, or who know for sure that an island lifestyle would never be for them. There are few people who are indifferent to the charms and history of Herm.

Perhaps the Perrys were inspired by Sir Compton Mackenzie, or the island simply triggered a desire to write. Whatever the reason the couple managed to capture something of the special atmosphere of Herm in their charming children's fairy story.

The fact that Perry, the wily businessman and chairman of the Ford Motor Company, felt able to put his name to a fairy story entitled The Island of Enchantment reveals a softer side to his nature. Herm must have been a good influence.

The couple co-wrote the fairy story about the 'litle island of Hame … between England and France', a colourful tale of a large family of children and the fairies who live on the island.

The adventures they have together involve Herm inspired dolphins, porpoises, (both of which were seen far more frequently in local waters in the 1920s compared to today) caves and caverns, puffins and crabs, limpets and congers and mentions by name Rosière Steps, Vermaret ("the lair of the Octopus Horde") a pine forest and a castle, Belvoir, and Valley Panto in a style reminiscent of J.M. Barrie's Peter Pan.

Something of their feelings about the relaxed, magical atmosphere of the island (and maybe the effect a stay had upon their friends!) is revealed by this passage:

"There were a number of Misters who came to play golf, but after they were shown to their rooms they were not seen again until a few days later, when they were discovered leaving the Channel island boat at Southampton; but out of their rooms came bounding Alfred, Billy, Ernest, Arthur, Jimmy, Andy, Jack, Dick and Bert; and as they remained on the island for several days and returned home again the very day the gentlemen were found, it can only be surmised that they were one and the same …"

"Yes!" the tale concludes, "*Hame is the land of the fairies*
You'll find out the farther you go,
On the beach you'll discover their clothing,
If you search when the tide is low."

The Island of Enchantment was published by Hutchinson and Co in the 1920s but there are only a handful of copies still in circulation. The Priaulx Library in Guernsey holds one copy and members of the library may borrow it.

The Dark Island by Vita Sackville West

Virginia and Leonard Woolf published Vita Sackville West's novel The Dark Island in 1934 a mysterious, strange story about the lives and loves of two women and a man, who live together in the castle of Storn. Some critics claim Storn to be Herm although Sackville West places her island off the coast of England (just as Mackenzie positions the fictional island of Roon in Fairy Gold).

The story revolves around the tormented Shirin who marries the dark and dangerously handsome Venn for his island rather than for her feelings for him. The third character is the strong and reliable Cristina, who also loves Shirin.

The book explores the lives of these three essentially tragic central figures. A fourth dominant influence is the island itself.

"She could see the island better now with its little harbour and fleet of shining boats, brightly painted idle in the sun, and the pink washed cottages whose green shutters gave them a curiously unEnglish appearance; and the ruddy mass of the Norman castle high above its terraces and the pine trees going down to the sea."

"... Storn to her was sacred, secret, set apart, it was like love, love which she had never known."

The story ends tragically – all three of the main characters die, one in a boating accident off a fictional islet.

The island is the only survivor, a strangely poetic place with great magnetism and mood, adorned with a beautiful beach, huge dark caves, a small jetty, and the pine clad hill leading to a castle.

Vita Sackville West may have got to know Herm when her brother Major General Charles Sackville was Governor General of Guernsey between 1925 and 1929 – also the time Compton Mackenzie was living in Jethou. It is conjecture, but I like to think the two writers met and that Mackenzie talked about his love affair with Herm and its mysteries which then went on to inspire the controversial novelist to write a book of her own based on the island.

The Mermaid of Herm a book of poems by Charles Clairmairis

Charles Clairmairis was inspired to write a short booklet of poems about Herm. In the foreword to his book he writes: *"... Herm's coastline possesses that mystic atmosphere which brings in its train art, literature, poetry and music ..."*

He dedicated his book of poems to The Mermaid of Herm – ..... *so that they may ultimately find themselves being sung where of course they should be – in the Mermaid Tavern!"*

Charles Clairmairis collaborated with Sir Compton Mackenzie in radio broadcasts about the Victorian and Edwardian periods before Mackenzie's move to Herm.

One of the amusing songs Clairmairis includes in his collection is entitled "There is a Barque down by the Quay", (to be sung, he instructs, in The Mermaid to the tune of "There is a Tavern in the Town") about the 'smugglers of Herm Island.'

(A copy of the booklet of poems can be found in the Priaulx Library)

Dorothy Osborne's Book of Letters:

"Do you remember Arme (Herm) and the little house there? Shall we go thither? That's next to being out of this worlde, there we may live like Baucis and Philemon, grow old together in our little cottage and for charity to some shipwrakt (sic) stranger obtaine the blessing of dying both at the same time."

This romantic passage was written by Dorothy Osborne, the daughter of the Governor of Guernsey Sir Peter Osborne to her future husband Sir William Temple and is often quoted.

Sir Peter Osborne became Governor of Guernsey in 1643, when Dorothy was just 16 years old. She was wooed by Henry Cromwell, the son of Oliver Cromwell, but Dorothy lost her heart to Sir William. During her father's governorship Dorothy and William visited Herm – her family were based in Castle Cornet and she must have enjoyed the views of Herm from the windows.

Which house could she be referring to? It was probably one of the early dwellings at the top of the hill.

At the time the island was privately annexed for the governors of the day, so the couple would have been able to spend romantic hours alone together on the island.

Dorothy Osborne was 27 when she wrote the lines on January 22, 1654. The story of Baucis and Philemon is in Ovid's Metamorphoses which was translated by George Sandys in 1626. It may have been this passage which she had in mind:

"A small thatched cottage where a pious wife,
Old Baucis and Philemon led their life.
Both equal aged. In this their youth they spent;
Who poverty, by bearing it, declined;
And made it easy with a cheerful mind.
None master, nor servant could you call;
They who command obey; for two were all."

In her letter Dorothy add:

"How idly I talk; tis because the story please me – none in Ovid so much. I remember I cried when I read it. Methought they were the perfectest characters of a contented marriage, where piety and love were all their wealth and in their poverty feasted the gods when rich men shut them out."

Tim Thompson – marine artist

Tim Thompson's fine works of art sell around the world. He specialises in painting ships and the sea, both historical and modern works in a fine, detailed style.

Tim Thompson lived on Herm between the ages of five and ten. His father was the island engineer, and his mother worked at the Shell Beach cafe during the summer season.

Thompson recalls spending hours gazing at the ever moving, ever changing sea swirling around the island, and having the freedom to explore – all the time never far from the sea, his inspiration. As a schoolboy on Herm he was always good at art.

Herm School has traditionally fostered a love of the natural world, and Thompson recalls occasions when school lessons were held on the beach. It was on Herm that he taught himself to paint and draw and as an adult developed a style that is now in demand from art collectors.

Herm Our Island Home by Jenny Wood

This is a delightful book which tells the story of the Wood family, who became Tenants of Herm in 1949. Jenny Wood's book is full of memories of the days when Herm was evolving into the haven that it has become today, and there is an emphasis on her own personal life story, the experience of bringing up six children on the island which in the beginning of their tenancy had no electricity, telephone or running water. Jenny Wood died in the summer of 1991.

Lord Perry's dream island
1923-1940

"I left school when I was 17 to start life with a little bicycle shop"
— Sir Percival Perry

Sir Percival Perry, later Lord Perry of Stock Harvard arrived in Herm waters aboard a friend's yacht in 1920 and immediately fell in love with the romantic notion of owning his own island. Three years later he realised his dream, buying the lease from Compton Mackenzie.

It was the start of another long tenancy which ended with the outbreak of the Second World War. Although he poured money into the island, and made improvements, there was very little long term reward.

At one stage Perry hoped to buy the freehold of the island from the Crown. But events conspired against him. In 1940 Herm, along with the other Channel Islands, was claimed as territory of the Third Reich.

The houses Perry had carefully restored and nurtured fell into a state of sad disrepair and neglect. Silver was looted and a battery powered electricity generator stolen by the Germans. Wine cellars were broken into.

After the war Perry's interest in Herm waned.

The States of Guernsey decided to buy the lease to Herm from the Crown in the hope of a better future, taking into account the opinion of local people – who felt strongly they wanted more access to this beautiful island, just as they had in Feilden's day.

Perry takes over

During his first walk upon the island shores in the company of Sir Compton Mackenzie, Perry made his interest in the island plain. He asked Mackenzie outright whether he might be interested in parting with the lease.

Perry was an astute businessman, and soon realised that Mackenzie was in financial difficulties. He used this to his advantage, offering Mackenzie a loan of £6,000 to be repaid in six monthly instalments which was to be devoted to improvements on the island. He hoped for a joint lease, to spread the cost of his investment.

According to his memoirs Mackenzie felt he had little choice but to accept this proposal which was not ideal, but at least allowed some breathing space for he was rapidly becoming short of cash.

Perry strung Mackenzie along refusing to give a date for taking up the option on the lease, but a year or so after their first meeting, Mackenzie discovered a loophole in their arrangement.

Perry had made provisions for bringing vehicles onto the island to help with clearance and to carry seaweed from the beaches to the fields, and to transport furniture on the island, but he had failed to make provision in the agreement for himself to stay on Herm. Mackenzie warned that unless he gave a date for taking up the option on the lease he would have to leave Herm immediately! Perry was forced to agree, and paid up and took over the whole lease to the island.

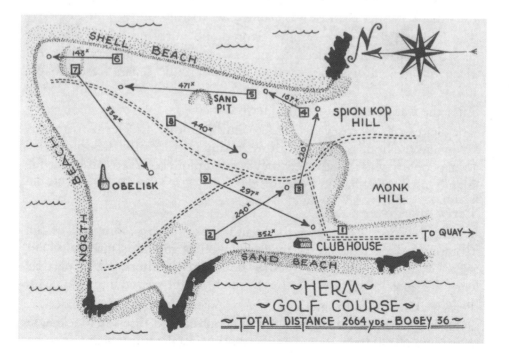

24 – The Golf Course built by Lord Perry on Herm Common.

25 – The arrival of a Ford Model T truck!

Herm improvements

During his tenancy the wealthy Perry, chairman of the Ford Motor Company in the UK and a director of the Firestone Tyre and Rubber Company, (as well as Henry Ford's right hand man) spent thousands of pounds on the island. Perry had made a name for himself as a businessman – in 1903 he imported the first Ford motor car into the UK from America, becoming Henry Ford's British agent. He set up the Ford Motor Company in Dagenham, a move that changed the face of modern car industry with the creation of the assembly line.

Meanwhile, he used Herm as a retreat to escape some of these work pressures, creating a fine country home for himself at The White House, installing the finest furniture, carpets, paintings and wall coverings from London and Europe.

He named his home The White House not just for its colour but also because of his American connections! (Perry also named the island pub The Mermaid Tavern).

In the early years of his tenancy he set about, with great enthusiasm, improving the island by planting 5,000 trees, restoring cottages, installing central heating in the White House, building a new inner harbour, tidying up the farm buildings (putting in the latest equipment in the milking stalls) and investing in a well managed farm stocked with pigs, poultry and 35 head of cattle.

His biggest problem was the booming rabbit population, and Perry found he needed to employ a full time trapper. Between 30 and 40 rabbits a day were sent to Guernsey market for sale.

At the height of his time on Herm Perry effectively created what the officials in Guernsey later described as a 'model tenancy'. Perry laid the foundations for a happy island kingdom, as the Blüchers had done before him but which Mackenzie had never been able to achieve.

There is no doubt that he managed Herm well, and enjoyed the island, but by the 1930s he rarely spent more than two months a year on Herm because of his heavy workload.

Instead he employed bailiffs, or island managers, to control his affairs, and to keep him posted on how the island was faring.

Fittingly, Perry was the first man to introduce motorised vehicles to the island – two ton Model T Ford trucks!

He employed a truck driver, as well as two engineers, one to look after matters at the bottom of the hill, and another for the 'top of the hill'.

A streak of eccentricity revealed itself when Perry insisted that virtually every visible surface be painted either blue or orange – blue was the colour of the Ford Motor Company's logo in Britain, while orange was originally the colour of Henry Ford's logo in America.

Perry sought special permission to paint the post box blue at the Tea Shop on the site of the present day Mermaid Tavern, as well as the outside of some buildings, gates, and the lamp posts he installed.

The most enduring story from his tenancy involved Perry's parrot, which was throttled to death one night by drunken staff. Perry installed a memorial to his parrot in the gardens behind the White House, which stands to this day hidden beneath the undergrowth of bushes and gorse. Herm also became a permanent home for some of his relatives – among them his three sisters in law. The women all lived in and around what was known then as the Mansion House (today's Manor House) which was made comfortable with modern heating, lighting, and fine bathrooms.

Oiling the wheels of business

Although Perry looked upon the island as an exclusive retreat he also found Herm useful for important 'networking'. Few could resist an invitation to stay on Perry's private island equipped with all mod cons. To help oil the wheels with his high flying guests he even built a golf course and golfing hut on The Common for their enjoyment, a plan of which hangs on the wall of The Mermaid Tavern. At traditional Christmas gatherings he would invite well connected guests to attend a fancy dress ball in The Mansion House, (presumably organised by the gaggle of female relatives). Tea dances were held once a fortnight. Film shows were held twice a week in the winter ... with Perry in charge, the island social life thrived.

In order to escape the endless wheeler-dealing that went on behind closed doors at the White House, Lady Catherine Perry found a quiet retreat for herself on the island.

She chose a delightful two-bedroomed cottage with a pretty garden and magnificent views across to Guernsey. This became known as Lady Perry's House, a name which is retained to this day as the home of Major Peter Wood.

When Major Wood became Tenant of Herm in 1949 he discovered the cottage hidden under a tangle of bramble and gorse, in a very dilapidated state.

He set about restoring, improving and extending the· cottage, which is now an extremely comfortable home, with huge picture windows. In Prince Blücher's era the cottage was used as a school.

26 – Lord Perry's opulent bedroom at The White House.

Meanwhile during summers on Herm Perry loved to indulge his passion for boating he owned four; a speedboat, a yacht and two cargo cum passenger boats. Henry Ford also enjoyed boats, and this probably led to him accepting Perry's invitation to stay in Belvoir House for a holiday one summer.

Perry's collection of boats prompted him to build the inner harbour and slipway, which exist and are used to this day. Edward Searson an employee of Perry's between 1930 and 1937, remembers seeing the harbour being built.

Seven workmen were employed on the job, and as a fitting memorial to Sir Percival Perry's tenancy, they placed the rusting remains of an old and disused Model T Ford truck into the cement structure of the harbour.

It remains there, buried in its concrete grave, a time capsule, awaiting the day it is 'rediscovered'.

The first flight to Herm

One of Perry's employees recalls the sale of one of the island's pedigree calves: it resulted in the arrival of an aristocratic contact flying into the island in his private plane and landing it on The Common!

While the aircraft was refuelled and the deal struck, Perry and his friend strolled along to the White House for refreshments before he returned to his parked craft which had been refuelled, to fly back to England complete with calf on board!

Perry employed 30 people on the island although there was no school during his tenancy. Once children reached the age of five the parents had to consider sending them to school in Guernsey or leaving their jobs on the island.

Perry allowed day visitors, but like his predecessors they had restricted access to the island, he preferred to keep Belvoir for his own use. Perry and his wife, Lady Catherine, must have enjoyed the relaxation and charm of the island; it came through in the children's fairy story they wrote together entitled The Island of Enchantment. (see page 72).

Perry allowed limited access to Herm to local visitors, as Mackenzie had done before him. As well as the tea shop for the visitors by The Mermaid Tavern, there was a bar, post office, and grocery shop for the island staff just along from the Mermaid Cottages.

Mr. Searson, who spoke to me in October 1995 aged 88, was employed as a truck driver and lived in Belvoir House between 1930 and 1937 with his wife and two small children. They were, he recalled with great clarity of mind, the happiest years of his life.

"As a truck driver my duties were to deliver coal on Thursdays and collect the dustbins on Fridays, to meet the boat every day and collect Lord Perry from the boat when he arrived on the island. I also repaired and maintained the roads around the island. I was paid 37/6 a week and was paid 1/6 by Lord Perry for any visitors who stayed at Belvoir House overnight – they might be the relatives of people living on the island. Dances were held every fortnight and on the first Saturday of the month country dances were held.

Whether Perry viewed Herm as his eventual retirement home (which is presumably why he wanted to buy the freehold) remains uncertain. But with the outbreak of war, and the loss of some of his wealth, his dreams for his island home faded fast.

He was unable to reach Herm during the war, and for some time before the outbreak of hostilities. In his last years as Tenant of Herm Perry was plagued with illness.

A demand for £450 in outstanding rent from the HM Receiver General in 1940 prompted Perry to explain that as Chairman of the Ford Motor Company he had accepted a reduction in his salary of £2,000 a year, and due to the war had lost income from his international investments. He had taken an unpaid voluntary job at the Ministry of Food and his income was severely cut.

When the war ended the Guernsey authorities decided that it would be in their best interests to buy the lease from the Crown and they set about finding a new tenant for the island as Perry's influence and interest in the island diminished.

The carefree island days of the 1920s and 1930s were gone forever. Once again it was a case of loving and then losing Herm. Perry, like others before him, found Herm to be a drain on his resources.

Perry set up another holiday home in the Bahamas, seeking out an island lifestyle but in a warmer climate. He died in 1956.

The occupation years

Herm was claimed by the Third Reich on July 20, 1940. As three uniformed Nazis arrived at Rosière Steps to occupy Herm there was just one man living alone on the island – all he could do was accept the arrival of the visiting soldiers.

That man was Frank Dickson who had been asked to look after Herm for a few days by Perry's last remaining employee on the island, Mr. Kemp, the caretaker.

Kemp made his way back to England – and was not heard of again in Herm. Meanwhile Frank Dickson was left to cope alone with the occupying forces who on that summer day consisted of the Oxford educated and meticulously polite Major Maass and two NCOs.

The Nazi major took an interest in the granite and shells of Herm, apparently he was a trained geologist. They set off back to Guernsey that evening, leaving Frank Dickson alone once more.

Soon he was joined by his wife Lil. Living on Herm was the rural idyll Frank Dickson had always dreamed of. But he did not bank on the occupying forces and to his credit made life as difficult as possible for the Germans at every opportunity. In return he was nicknamed by the Germans as the "Robinson Crusoe" of Herm.

During the first months of the occupation the Dicksons were left very much to their own devices.

There would be visits by German officers and their girlfriends and shooting parties hoping to bag pheasants or rabbits.

The peacefulness of the island was shattered in September 1940 when the Germans carried out a seaborne mock 'invasion' of Herm using infantry posted in Guernsey. The whole operation was filmed and used for propaganda purposes back in Germany – the film was entitled The Invasion of the Isle of Wight.

In March 1941 the Dicksons were joined for a month by their 17 year old nephew Martin Le Page.

When I interviewed Mr. Le Page in 1995 aged 71 he told me: "To me watching Guernsey slip behind, was like travelling to another world."

Life in Herm in those years of occupation did in fact turn out just like that – it offered a complete contrast to what was going on in Guernsey. It was very much a rural existence, trapping rabbits, milking the cow, tending the vegetable patch, collecting limpets for the chickens to eat, and gathering gulls' eggs.

In 1942 Frank and Lil Dickson were joined by Martin Le Page's parents, Ernest and Daisy Le Page, who were appointed to look after a flock of 60 sheep. The Le Page family moved into Laranda cottage just above the harbour, which had been used by members of Perry's staff only a few years earlier.

Almost as soon as they had settled in, the Dicksons were ordered to leave for Guernsey – Frank Dickson had made himself unpopular with the German soldiers and the occupying commandant got 'his own back' by telling him to leave the island.

This left the Le Pages alone on Herm although they were later joined by Rose Clifford, a house keeper from Guernsey, and Martin Le Page visited regularly.

"*Herm offered the chance of escape from the pressures of living with the Germans in Guernsey. There was complete freedom from all the military restrictions,*" he said.

The Le Pages also learned to put up with the visiting Germans. They would come to search island buildings or use The Common for target practise.

A battery of German soldiers moved into Herm but their occupation only lasted a matter of

27 – Lord Perry of Stock Harvard.

weeks. These soldiers were probably responsible for shooting down one of their own planes which crashed near Belvoir (a wing tip was found on the beach). A few days later the German soldiers were recalled to Guernsey to who knows what fate! They left much barbed wire around the south coast and a sign warning that the cliffs had been mined.

In February 1943 a party of seven British Commandos and Royal Marines made a daring raid on Herm in the middle of the night under the command of Captain Patrick Porteous, VC.

The men landed on Herm in the pitch dark on board a 14 foot dory which had to be paddled to the shore. Their objectives were to discover whether Shell Beach was mined, to locate the watch tower and capture a guard (there wasn't one) and to distribute aircraft leaflets, thereby confusing the Germans.

The party also checked out the Manor House, and as they found the cottages and house empty they stole away again into the night. (Coincidentally one of the men working on some of the Channel Island war time operations was Major Geoffrey Appleyard – the brother of Mrs. Jenny Wood, who a few years later would make Herm her home.)

After D-Day the Le Pages were joined by the Macdonalds who were the caretakers in Jethou and had been employed by Sir Compton Mackenzie. Eleven days before the final liberation of the islands the families were joined by a forlorn looking German officer who had been exiled to Herm from Guernsey. He moved into The Manor but was rarely seen out and about on the island. It turned out that he was opposed to Hitler's fortress policy.

On May 9 1945 the liberating forces could be seen in the Little Russell from Herm. Mrs. Le Page found a small Union Jack and made her way to the harbour. A young German soldier approached, saluted and took the flag. He climbed to the top of the railway crane and attached the flag. Not a word was spoken – none were necessary. It was the end of the occupation of Herm.

Martin Le Page has written a book about his war time experiences and life on Herm during the occupation years, entitled A Boy Messenger's War.

*The inner harbour

* The former golf course on The Common
(see map in the Mermaid Tavern)

* Parrot Memorial behind White House Hotel

* Lady Perry's House, the present day home of
Major Peter Wood, who became Tenant of Herm in 1949

*The White House – named by Lord Perry

* The hotel cottage, Laranda, was named after
Lord Perry's favourite yacht

*Belvoir House, used as a holiday retreat by Henry Ford,
the US car magnate.

Modern Times
1945 to the present day

"Propitiate at all costs the spirits of the island" –
- Mrs. Faith Compton Mackenzie.

After the war

On May 20th, 1945 Lt. Col K.H.H. Allen, of 20 Civil Affairs Unit, Guernsey filed a report on the conditions on Herm at the end of the Second World War. He found one horse and five residents on the island (including the Macdonalds who asked to be allowed to return to Jethou), one cow, 31 sheep and a few chickens.

In addition there were 22 beds 'used by the Germans' about 200 rounds of ammunition, wood felling equipment and 20 tons of pine wood cut into three foot lengths ready for shipment.

Lt Col Allen asked for a tractor and 20 men to work on a 'clearance operation' for several days and concluded. "As far as is known mines have been removed and there are no fortifications though there is some wire." In July 1946 the States of Guernsey debated whether to buy Herm. In December the deal was struck – the island was bought from the Crown for £15,000.

The States resolved that the governing principle should be to ensure 'that the natural attractions and peacefulness of the island are preserved and made available to all who visit it."

The late Jurat Sir John Leale who made the proposal said: "I don't want to be met by the blare of a merry go round when I land in Herm."

It was agreed that the island should be preserved 'for all time in its natural state, for the enjoyment of all wishing to land there.'

The Board of Administration was entrusted – and still is – with ensuring that this policy was carried out and given the job of choosing suitable tenants and arranging for an 'appropriate lease'.

Before the formal purchase, an advertisement was placed in The Times in October 1946 inviting applications for the tenancy of Herm. A shortlist of four applicants was drawn up.

Amongst the proposals were plans for a " Recuperative Health Centre" from a team of doctors and a surgeon, who considered "the climate of Herm being exceptionally warm yet invigorating, … as being ideal for people recovering from illness and in general those in need of rest, simple living in healthy surroundings and good food."

The Manor, it was suggested, would be 'entirely devoted' to a well equipped clinic for convalescent patients where dietetic, electro-physical and hydro-therapy treatments would be available.

The plan was rejected – but imagine the consequences if it had not been – The Herm Health Farm.

Another applicant wanted to turn Herm into a holiday camp with chalets dotted around the island – this also failed to make the grade.

John Tindal Woodward of Park Crescent, London, an applicant on the shortlist, was on the right lines when he proposed to turn The White House into a 'first class hotel' with a 'first class ballroom'.

He suggested a fisherman's bar, the restoration of the nine hole golf course, installing a large electricity power plant. Perhaps the fact that he wanted to keep one of the bays for his own personal use finally went against him!

The man who eventually became the first Tenant of Herm appointed by Guernsey was Mr. A. G. Jefferies, a retired glove manufacturer who had employed 1,000 people in seven factories. His suggestion that he would develop the island "slowly and soundly so that the Island of Herm will eventually become a high class holiday resort in keeping with past and present Guernsey standards" appealed to the Board of Administration.

A tenancy agreement between Jefferies and the Board was drawn up during 1946 – he was given full responsibility for putting the whole island including the buildings into proper order as well as allowing the public free access during the hours of daylight.

Just one year later Jefferies realised that he could not run Herm profitably under the terms of the lease. He asked for permission to levy a landing charge of 1/- which was agreed, although Jefferies only received a quarter of the payment.

By 1949 Jefferies found it impossible to run Herm – he was, by now well into his 50s and there was a lot of hard, physical work to be done restoring the buildings and setting up the island businesses.

One of the interesting legacies from his short tenancy, however, was the creation of a pigeon postal service which ran from Herm to a loft in St. Peter Port.

Coincidentally Jefferies met Major Peter Wood and his wife Jenny and told them of his 'ownership of an island'. When they heard it was for sale, the couple flew off to view the island. It was love at first sight. In July of that year Major and Mrs. Wood became the new Tenants of Herm – despite earnest opposition from family and financial advisors! It was the start of another chapter in the history of the island.

The Guernsey phone box which the Woods used to say they wanted to take on the island was later bought by the couple and stands as a memento of that day in the playground of Herm School in the Manor Village.

28 – Those were the days! The Mermaid Tavern – as it was.

Major Wood set up the Herm postal service, and at 4.55pm on June 9th 1950 was present when the first telephone call was made between Herm and Guernsey. In the 1970s Major Wood oversaw the building of the new Herm dairy farm, the first development on the island outside the two 'village areas'. The farm buildings were deliberately sunk low into the landscape and replaced the barns and dairy parlours in the Manor courtyards which had been used up until that time.

The story of the Wood's life laying the foundations of Herm as it is today, is eloquently told in the book, *Herm Our Island Home* written by Jenny Wood.

She tells of the early, hard years before her husband and his brother, Philip Wood, installed water, electricity, and telephones on the island and explains how the island businesses were developed.

The book is available from the Herm Gift Shops.

Herm today

Few people have succeeded in living happily on an island – and making the whole enterprise work, and prosper, into the bargain. Major Peter Wood and members of his family rank among this minority.

Herm as it exists and is managed today is a direct result of nearly half a century of hard work by the Wood family. There is a scheme to the island, a framework and routine that has, over the years, been refined, and is still evolving.

The island employs over 50 permanent staff, most with young families, which helps to create a community atmosphere. There is a primary school, and a full time schoolmistress employed by the Guernsey education authority.

Most of the permanent staff are recruited from the mainland UK. A rural background is not a requirement, so Herm has allowed city dwellers from London, Birmingham, Manchester, and other major centres the opportunity to experience this unique island lifestyle. There are no requirements for housing licences on Herm, as in other Channel Islands. However, residency of the island lasts only as long as the job – so there are no retired members of staff on the island, and no ageing population. Life on Herm today means being able to accept that your working and home life are inextricably linked which is rare. Some employees find this hard to manage and leave after a few short months. Others settle down to enjoy life in idyllic surroundings with a ready made community on tap and plenty of work all year round.

As one of those residents I can only tell you of my personal views on island life. There is an appeal in every season of the year. The long warm sunny days of summer gradually melt into the invigorating, fresher autumn months when the colours of the island take on a golden and amber hue.

In winter the sense of being apart from the mainland is enhanced by the enjoyment of a real log fire and hearing the wind whistle and echo through the pine trees.

Spring is a sheer delight when the island bursts into a bloom of colour and the promise of summer is captured in the scented, warm air. These impressions must have been shared by every passing resident with a sensitivity to their surroundings, and the appeal is timeless.

This lifestyle is lost elsewhere: the island provides a unique, safe and beautiful environment for children who can play freely, as well as enjoying a healthy, and pollution free atmosphere.

29 – Copy of the document required to travel between Guernsey and Herm during the occupation years.

As the rest of the United Kingdom complains about the size of classrooms, the violence of society, the anonymity of city life, and the dangers of drugs, Herm stands out as something different, unique, amidst the chaos of modern life.

Life is governed by tides and weather – in the middle of winter appointments may have to be missed, so a philosophical attitude is needed.

Some might say it is escapism, but for those of us who live here, it becomes another way of life, one hard to duplicate elsewhere. Visitors to the island get a chance to sample this lifestyle, as invariably during their stay they become 'adopted' islanders and may find they are asked to lend a hand, carrying milk churns up Rosière Steps, or unloading boxes from the latest delivery of cargo!

Present Day Management

The Wood family have held the lease for the longest period of time since the rule of the Norman churches. It is almost as if Herm had been waiting to share her natural treasures, for there is an air of peacefulness and harmony. This sense of peacefulness encourages visitors to return, time after time.

In 1987 the tenancy of the island was changed to a new and unique position. The lease was extended – it now runs until the year 2049 – and transferred to a company, Wood of Herm Island.

This company is owned entirely by members of Major Wood's family, with the intention that the lease of the island is retained for future generations.

Adrian Heyworth, the present island manager, is chairman of the company and, together with his wife Pennie, (Major Wood's daughter) the couple are the 'hands on' managing directors, responsible for the appointment of staff and the day to day running of the island.

Adrian became Island Manager in 1980 at the age of 28 after training in estate management. Under his and Pennie's direction Herm has established a secure financial footing, probably the best in its long and varied history. The island is prospering, and the tormented years when tenants faced bankruptcy and ruin are now over.

31 and 32 – Trees and birds on Herm.

95

The Heyworths have created a healthy financial position, as well as considerably improving the island, for visitors and those who live here. The legacy of the Heyworth era will be the upgrading of many island buildings and the creation of ongoing conservation programmes to save the shifting sand dunes to the north and west of the island, and restoration of the woodlands. Above all the couple have a desire to retain the natural peacefulness of the island, and this is reflected in all their policies. Pennie Heyworth, who was born in Lady Perry's House in November 1950, is a keen conservationist with an interest in plant and bird life of the island.

Herm Island lies to the west of Guernsey opposite St. Peter Port Harbour and just 20 miles from the nearest point of France. There is a boat service every day of the year from St. Peter Port to Herm, apart from Christmas Day or when there are adverse weather conditions.

* Boats land at Herm Harbour in the three hours before and after high tide. In the three hours before and after low tide boats moor at Rosière Steps, a flight of 41 steps leading to a granite archway. (There are 41 steps when you alight from the ferry and take the left hand walkway, and 47 steps if you follow the right hand walkway.)*

* Well signed coastal pathways lead visitors around the island. To the north are the beaches, to the south the cliff pathways. (See page 111 for suggested walks and what to look for en route.)*

* Herm Island is one and a half miles long by half a mile wide. It has some of the largest tidal flows of anywhere in the world. The large spring tides almost double the size of the island.*

* The island has three diesel generators producing a maximum of 130 kilowatts.*

* There are four water bore holes providing the island with its water supply.*

* The main industries are tourism and farming. There is a herd of 60 pedigree cows on the island.*

For further information about the facilities on Herm contact the Administration Office and ask for an island brochure and tariff.

During their management Adrian has overseen the extensions to The Mermaid Tavern, The White House Hotel, renovation of hotel cottage bedrooms, the creation of new self catering apartments and cottages from the frame of existing, derelict buildings, improvements to the campsites, upgrading of public utilities, and in 1995 major alterations to the Rosière Steps which made this landing area more accessible for the visitors to the island.

Over 14,000 trees have been planted on the island during the Heyworth era.

From 1945 onwards

* Enlargement to Hotel

* Redevelopment of manor village and harbour village

* Creation of campsites and self catering cottages

* Development of tourist amenities

* Tree planting

* Restoration of all main buildings

* Creation of shopping piazza

* Improvements to Rosière Steps

* Creation of 19 self-catering cottages and apartments for use by holidaymakers

* Development of campsite amenities

Folklore of Herm

"Pirates gibbeted along the northern shore, Celtic princes buried in those great Cromlechs, bygone generations of dreamers, malefactors, lovers, mariners, witches, monks, prehistoric men and women, they have all left something of themselves behind."

– Sir Compton Mackenzie .

If we knew everything about Herm from the moment Mesolithic people first stepped ashore much of the romanticism of the island would be lost forever.

History is ingrained in the tough pink and grey granite, and seeps out of every nook and cranny. Part of the charm of the island is to walk and conjure up images of past times and lifestyles.

There is a benign air of mystery – it seems as if the weight of the island's history is carried in the air. Surprisingly large numbers of people comment upon the island's distinctive atmosphere.

Many have attempted to capture the sense of Herm's mystical qualities. Jenny Wood, in her book, talks of the lower slopes of Petit and Grand Monceau being 'strangely disquieting'.

"Although I love most of The Common," she writes, "this particular place has to me a strange haunted air as if great emotions have been roused here at some time, and which still linger to charge the atmosphere with their presence."

Miss Edith Carey in her book The Channel Islands talks of Herm possessing 'elemental powers which resent the intrusion of human personality' which seems a fairly dramatic statement in the light of the enjoyment the island now gives to so many thousands of people each year!

Vita Sackville West captures some of the mysticism in her mysterious book The Dark Island, in which the moods of her mythical island, Storn, (apparently based on Herm) are atmospherically described, in particular the thunder storms which can dramatically hit the Channel Islands when high and low pressures collide.

Sir Compton Mackenzie, who loved Herm, but found the island too costly to keep, also wrote of his deep feelings that it was a haunted island.

The only time he experienced 'deep authentic panic', he wrote, was when he was looking for moths and mushrooms one breathless autumn evening near the Neolithic tombs on the common.

"Suddenly I became aware of elemental spirits all round me and I ran a mile to the safety of glimmering cottage windows."

Herm's ghosts:

One of the stories island residents soon get to hear about is the alleged ghost of Herm – the apparition of a monk in a long dark cloak. He is said to stroll in Valley Panto, and many people have independently felt a strange sensation walking up The Drive at night without light to guide them.

It may be fanciful imagination, but Herm has been home to so many people with strong wills, and strong feelings that I tend to agree with Sir Compton Mackenzie who said: "Yes, Herm was (and probably still is) a haunted island."

Prince Blücher's farm bailiff, Mr. Harding, who lived on Herm for over 50 years, recalls hearing occasionally a 'terrifying roar' generally on a very still frosty night.

In the early 1900s he was trapping rabbits at 1am on a January morning; it was absolutely still and there was not a breath of wind.

In the transactions of La Société Guernesiaise the story continues:

"Suddenly the willow tree under which he stood, situated in the north of the island, bowed over and seemed to bow to the ground and then came an indescribable noise which seemed to rush past him like a wind. It lasted about a minute or so and then, quivering with fright, Harding went home."

Tom le Pelley who worked in Herm as a gardener in the early 1800s also heard this noise, according to old papers.

Were these the same elemental forces that Sir Compton Mackenzie also experienced? Or was it simply some natural phenomenon, such as the sound of the sea roaring through an opening in the rocks, or via some other geological formation?

(Herm once possessed a huge cave, the Creux du Pignon, which extended upwards to a cliff top shaft in the south part of the island. The creux has since collapsed. The sound of the sea and wind blown upwards through this type of natural opening can create eery noises.) Officers posted to Herm with the Staffordshire Light Infantry during the First World War sensed something 'other worldly' about Herm, and recorded the fact that their men would only patrol the island in pairs, and never alone. But this might have had more to do with the remaining wallabies on the island who would lope along the road making odd noises with their feet.

When a new heating system was being installed at St. Tugual's Chapel a hole was dug outside the chapel door – the entrance is off the Manor courtyard. Workmen found the skeleton of a man buried upright, as though he had been standing, directly in front of the door. Was this the monk – buried outside the door of the church, and not allowed in – had he been punished for some misdemeanour? The answer to that mystery will never be known.

More recently staff at the Mermaid Tavern have heard strange noises after midnight on winter's evenings, and there have been incidence of candles relighting themselves, and bottles falling from shelves without warning or reason.

33 – Shell illustrations, Scallop shells.

Similar stories are told at the hotel – on one occasion the sound of someone brushing out a fire grate was heard coming from one of the lounges. When the door to the lounge was opened no-one was there.

The Island Cemetery:

A photograph of the little cemetery found at the end of Fisherman's Path was taken in the 1880s and is lodged in the Priaulx Library.

Today the inscription reads: In Memory of K.W. Conden aged 2 years and R. Mansfield aged 33 years died April 1832 Rest in peace."

With a magnification of 200 the age for Conden reads as 22. The rest is very hazy – the month is certainly April, the date unclear.

One theory is that these two young people were victims of cholera, that a ship travelling from Jersey was unable to off load the corpses and they were buried in Herm. This seems unlikely for it would have been during the quarrying days in Herm, when the island had a large working population.

A story that has persisted since Victorian times is that it is the grave of two men who drowned after an accident at sea. In 1858 two adults were drowned in the small rocky passage between Herm and Jethou. In 1873 The Ranger, a ship owned by Col Feilden – the brandy smuggler – sank off Herm, and was lost. Col Feilden's son, who lived in Guernsey, and who lived on Herm as a boy told a newspaper reporter that two men were drowned in this incident, and that this was their grave.

Further weight is given to this theory by a report in the transactions of La Société Guernesiaise of an outing to Herm on July 7 1916 – members were told it was the grave of two young men who died by drowning.

Dr. Stanley Kellet Smith conducted a long search of official records and documents but could find no reference to two young men of this name, who died in the 1800s. Who they were, and how they died, is one of the island's enduring mysteries.

Slaughter of Roman Catholics:

When Henry VIII created the new Church of England he urged the 'monkish tenants' of the Channel Islands to conform. One legend has it that all the Roman Catholics fled to Herm and attempted to hold out against the onslaught of the Calvinists. Most of the 400 refugees were slaughtered here.

However, there is only little evidence that this happened – one article in La France Illustrée in the 19th century makes the claim, so until further proof comes to light, must remain another legend of Herm.

The shells of Shell Beach:

The shells found on this beach are one of the star attractions of the island. For generations people have walked and collected the assortment of coloured shells – many of which are so tiny that amateur conchologists need to get down on their hands and knees to discover the treasure. But how do these extraordinary beautiful shells come to be washed up on the shores of Herm?

Jill Kendrick who has studied the island shells, and written a book about 50 of the different types, believes that all the molluscs which once occupied the shells comes from local waters, and it is the combination of tidal flows which has helped the waters around the island to create the right environment for such a collection of molluscs.

Famous avid collectors of Herm shells were the late Lord Bath, and Lady Bath, who used to holiday annually on the island. The couple picked up hundreds of tiny pink cowrie shells on their trips, and upon their return to Longleat House in Wiltshire stored them in three foot high glass apothecary jars.

34 – Shell illustrations, Common Wentletrap.

The shell jars have become prized family possessions, and are displayed prominently in the Old Library at Longleat. This part of the house is not open to the public, as it is part of the family's private apartments.

Barbara's Leap:

There really was a Barbara who leaped off this dangerous cliff on the south coast ... It is safely fenced off now, but in the 1950s, when the incident happened, it was more open. Barbara worked on the island, and was suffering from a broken romance when she threw herself down the cliffs. She survived, and after medical attention returned to live on the island.

The Natural Life

"The birds on an island like Herm are even more delightful than the birds of the mainland because one gets to know them individually"

– Sir Compton Mackenzie

Birds

Herm can be relied on for some exciting birding – in winter the Brent geese; in spring the puffins; in summer, the gannets; and autumn the visiting migrants from as far away as South Africa.

The geology of Herm affects its botany, insects and, therefore, its birdlife. The southern cliffs are 2,500 million years old. The northern deposits of glacial sand that form The Common are probably less than 10,000 years old.

Before the Atlantic Ocean was formed the sea level was much higher than today and the top of Herm, at 60 metres, is a wave cut platform, formed when Guernsey and Herm were still part of mainland Europe.

As the Atlantic formed so the sea levels dropped and the islands were raised hills in a larger landscape. They were cut off from the mainland by the action of vast melt water rivers that came off the ice caps that extended down to The Thames during the four great Ice Ages that spanned the period 2 million – 10,000 BC.

Birds are known to date from 40 million years ago – which certainly puts human beings into perspective, as we only date back 2 million years or so! Resident birds on Herm include the kestrel, the commonest bird of prey. The male has a grey head and rump, the larger female is brown over head, back and rump. They, like the long eared owls breed on the island, feeding on the mice and shrews that shelter in the stone walls. Robins, wrens, dunnocks, blackbird and song thrushes all breed here. In winter local numbers are swelled by visitors from central and northern Europe.

The red wing and fieldfare visit from Scandinavia in winter as well as mistle thrushes, great tits and blue tits, chaffinches, and greenfinches.

Around the coast the black and white oystercatcher with its bright carrot coloured bill is always heard, joined in the winter by curlew and turnstone, (the Bailiwick is a site of international importance for turnstone).

The 'mewing' of the herring gull can be heard all year round – other residents include the lesser and great black backed gulls and black headed gulls.

Up to 100 Brent geese are usually seen around Bear's Beach between October and April when they leave to return to the Arctic Coast of Siberia. From December you can see the earliest gannets fishing at sea. Great northern and black throated divers have been recorded as have great crested and red necked grebes. Pure white little egrets are increasing in numbers spreading west from France. They join their cousins, the grey herons, for winter here.

Spring is probably the best time for seeing birds. Migrants from Southern Europe, and Africa join resident birds to feed. From Herm they will move north into the UK, and Scandinavia.

The puffins are here every spring, although their numbers are declining. They can be seen off the south east coast of Herm from March to July nesting in old rabbit burrows or, occasionally, under larger rocks. They lay a single white egg in April.

Their cousins in the auk family, the guillemot and razorbill can also be found around Jethou and Grand Fauconnière (Falcon Rock – so named because kestrels bred here in the 16th century).

Common terns flying in from South and West Africa nest off the east coast of Herm.

Flying over land are the house martins, swallows, and later on swifts. On The Common the cuckoo will be calling from May onwards. The meadow pipits are numerous at this time of year flying over The Common.

The gorse bushes provide song perches for migrant whinchat, whitethroat, chiff-chaff and willow warbler. In wooded areas look for pied flycatchers in April and May also common redstarts, woodwarblers, wheatears and even grasshopper warblers.

At this time of year the male wren will be building up to six different nests for his mate to choose from.

In the wooded areas you should find the rare goldcrest, and short-toed treecreeper.

Around the coast look for the stunning grey plovers, the smaller dunlin, and the ringed plover, one of the Bailiwick's scarcest breeding birds. Shags, cormorants, and fulmar petrels, will all be breeding and have nests around the cliffs and coast.

In the autumn, birds are on the move again. Travelling south this time are the sanderling, knot and curlew sandpiper.

September is the month for the tiny little stint which looks like a miniature dunlin. Yellow-browed warblers from Siberia also stop off in Herm. The commonest migrants seen in the spring will be returning to the island such as warblers and flycatchers.

When the Brent geese return in October you know the bird watching year has come full circle.

(With special thanks to Tony Grange)

Plant Life:

Records of plant life on Herm go back 200 years – in 1837 the first full list of plants on the island was published, and 174 species were listed. Today the list of plants extends to more than 450.

Here are a few of the more interesting plants to be found on Herm contained in a brief check list.

Spring

The Common:

Bracken; daisy; dark mouse ear; thyme-leaved sandwort; fairyflax; salad burnet; sharp rush; ladies bedstraw which contains an agent used as an anti-coagulant; marram grass, planted along the top of Shell Beach to prevent erosion; burnet rose; sand sedge.

Cliff paths:

The most interesting is Nottingham catchfly which attracts moths, flowers best in the evening and is not found in Guernsey; foxgloves; ground ivy, which was used before hops to make beer, one of the chief agents in flavouring and clarifying ale; bluebells; sea campion; sea pinks/ thrift; forget-me-nots; hogweed.

Elsewhere:

Bermuda buttercup; Royal Fern planted on the pathway between Belvoir Bay and Shell Beach; lesser celandine; hemlock – the plant that killed Socrates, and which the Greeks used to mix a fatal cocktail administered

35 – Sheil beach at the turn of the century

as a 'death penalty', can be mistaken for hogweed or alexanders; wild garlic – a very pungent smell; primrose; wild leek; Guernsey star of Bethlehem (The Drive); gladdon or stinking iris, also on The Drive.

Summer

The Common:

Rest harrow a plant which anchors in the sand; sweet briar which has the smell of apples; viper's bugloss, attracts bees and burnet moths; lesser calamint, autumn squill which look like tiny bluebells, thyme and birds foot trefoil.

The Cliffs:

Sea campion; red campion which has the local name of 'soldier's fleas' because of the black aphids which are attracted to the plant in summer; bell heather, sea fig.

Beaches:

Sea rocket (the seeds float); sea bindweed; sea holly which binds the sand with penetrating fleshy roots which were used to make candied sweetmeats in the Elizabethan age; sea knotgrass which is a very rare plant and only exists in dunes which are stabilising; New Zealand flax and marram grass.

Elsewhere

Balm leaved figwort is found at the top of Rosière Steps, it is rare in the UK but common in Channel Islands; reeds at the top of the Fisherman's Beach will only grow in freshwater, so indicate a freshwater spring.

In the Autumn look out for slender fuchsia; ivy, the last British plant to flower and found all over the island, most particularly along Fisherman's Path – it attracts a great many insects; autumn cyclamen on the south side of The Drive, and the fruits of blackberry, sloe and elderberry.

(With special thanks to Rachel Rabey and Jenny Le Huquet)

For further information about the plant and bird life on Herm contact La Société Guernesiaise or ask at the Herm Gift Shops for specialist publications.

The Good Beach Guide

There are eight highly individual, accessible beaches on Herm – quite a record for an island of just 500 square acres. Most people agree they are the finest beaches to be found anywhere in the Channel Islands.

Hotel Beach:

Convenient for White House Hotel guests – quiet, secluded spots can be found to the south of the beach. May be overlooked by visitors returning from the harbour. Soft, golden sand in its favour.

Harbour Beach:

Can be busy at the height of the summer, but convenient for boaters. Also handy if you don't have much time and still want to allow children to play on sand. Boulders are a great natural playground for the young at heart.

Fisherman's Beach:

Just below Fisherman's Path, the beach can be reached by scrambling over rocks from the neighbouring Harbour Beach or down steps, found a few yards along from The Mermaid Tavern.

The great joy of this beach is at low tide when hundreds of rock pools are exposed, which keep children entertained for hours in their search for starfish, crabs, small fish and other varied sea life. At high tide sunbathers can enjoy the activity at the harbour and it is only a short way to walk to reach the sea for a swim.

Good for Families * * * * *

Bear's Beach:

Named by Major Wood whose six children particularly enjoyed playing on this huge expanse of golden sand with an imaginary family of bears.

A delightful beach for sun worshippers, families, or those seeking seclusion. There is so much room that you can still find a quiet spot on the busiest day. Ideal for evening barbecues, and there are plenty of safe, flat rocks for children to play on. Not ideal for swimming at low tide as the sea level falls dramatically.

Oyster Point:

Wins top marks for seclusion and escapism. There are plenty of shells on this beach which makes for an interesting afternoon. Rocks at the north end provide cover from the northerly winds. An attractive sand dune backdrop which fall to a beach which is bleached white by the sun. It takes a bit of time to find the beach for the first time, but is well worth the march through prickly hawthorn bushes and spiky marram grass!
Seclusion * * *

Shell Beach:

The most famous Herm beach and therefore the most popular. Some visitors walk to the beach and never leave until it is time for their ferry to depart! Almost three quarters of a mile of golden sand and small, beautiful shells. The sea here is ideal for swimming at both high and low tide. The sand is clean – make sure you get down on hands and knees to find the prettiest shells. Don't expect to come to the beach and wade ankle high through large shells.
Best of everything* * * * *

Belvoir Bay:

Small but beautifully formed. In the shoulder months of June and September it is an ideal spot as it is far less crowded than during July and August. Perfect for swimming and children – safe, clear, shallow waters. Also a wonderful bracing place for fresh winter days: virgin golden sand crunches underfoot as the green-blue sea rushes in.

Most serious sunbathers head for Belvoir in the height of the summer.
Sunbathing, swimming and beauty * * * * *

North Beach:

One of the least used, but most fascinating beaches on the island. You can find a sunny secluded spot, plenty of rock pooling, shells, and a quite different outlook compared to other beaches.

It is long and varied, and at high tide there are some excellent spots for shallow swimming. Beware of tidal currents further out.
Something different * * *

Walks on Herm

The Harbour to Belvoir Bay via The Drive

The harbour lies on the west of the island, and is used by the ferries coming to Herm in the three hours before, and three hours after, high tide. The granite built harbour was built in the mid 1800s and improved gradually over the following 50 years. In the 1930s Sir Percival Perry, later Lord Perry, built the inner harbour and slipway for his collection of four boats.

Look for the upside down cannon, now used as a mooring point. The Bray Waddington railway crane dominates the harbour scene: there are some 70 yards of rail still in place on the harbour – the gauge is an unusual size, four foot five and three quarter inches. This is the original track used to transport granite from the quarries to the harbour.

The line veers off to the right towards Rosière, and the first quarry on the island, now covered by undergrowth, behind the hotel.

At the roundabout (nicknamed Piccadilly Circus by locals) there are three possible routes.

To the right is the hotel and a lower pathway leading to Rosière Steps and the south of the island, to the left is the path that leads past the shopping piazza designed and built by Italian craftsmen in the 1950s, and further on The Mermaid Tavern. Beyond that is the route above Bear's Beach and Fisherman's Beach and on towards Shell Beach.

The third route lies directly in front, beyond the two granite pillars which were built in the early 1900s for Prince Blücher who turned Herm into his personal private kingdom, complete with a castle. Two large gates were once hung from the pillars preventing visitors from straying onto the private part of the island.

Step beyond the two pillars and enter The Drive a steep but pretty climb, to the top of the island. On the left is Harbour Cottage, one of the earliest buildings on Herm. To the right are other cottages dating back almost 200 years originally built for quarrymen.

The cottage named Foxglove was used as the first school on Herm. There are magnificent views from The Drive over the harbour and out towards Fisherman's Cottage, the small white cottage which nestles in the valley below Monku. Look out for another, less attractive pair of stone gateposts half way up the hill, and just beyond them the island water station, and behind that a small reservoir.

A wooden gate on the right leads into Valley Panto, named after a mediaeval monk. The sleeping policemen, or stone humps, were laid down in the 1930s.

As the road turns to the left New Zealand flax, planted by Sir Compton Mackenzie in the 1920s, on the right towers above other flowering plants.

Further on, to the right, is a shaded wood area, which in the spring bursts into bloom with a host of magnificent bluebells.

The overhanging trees on this part of the walk provide welcome respite from the hot sunshine during the summer months.

Almost at the top of the hill, on the right partially hidden by trees and bushes are granite walls which surround the private part of the island. These walls were also built in Prince Blücher's era; note the castellated effect.

A white door in the wall on the right leads to Lady Perry's House and is also an entrance to the garden of The Manor.

The next turning to the right leads to St. Tugual's Chapel, the 11th century chapel which today contains some stunning stained glass windows.

To the left is a magnificent view across Herm Harbour to Guernsey. Follow the path past self catering cottages which were once original dairy and farm buildings. Around the corner is another large barn used by the Herm Oyster Farm for grading the shellfish.

Next door to this barn is the island power station.

At the end of the path turn right, then immediately left to take the stony track to Belvoir Bay. This branches off The Spine Road, one of the oldest paths on the island. Dry stone walls are a feature of the path, and may have been originally built for the Norman monks who lived on the island in the Dark Ages.

Drystone Walls

To the South Coast

THE DRIVE

To Belvoir

To the Common

SPINE ROAD

Prince Blücher's Gate Posts

Oxen Shoeing Stocks

113

Further south along the Spine Road just above the turning to Belvoir are the oxen shoeing stocks.

The track to Belvoir Bay winds steeply through a lovely undulating valley, with green fields to the right. Look for the magnificent Monterey pines another signature from the Blücher period.

Belvoir House nestles in the valley; the lower part is the home of an island resident and the top part is let as a self catering apartment.

The path slopes down through newly planted copses of oak and evergreen trees until it divides into three – to the right is the path to Rosière, to the left is the pathway to The Common.

The middle path leads down to Belvoir Bay, one of the finest coves on the island, and the most popular for swimming and sunbathing in the summer. This was once Princess Wanda Blücher's private beach – and no wonder! A small cafe provides refreshments and there are views across the water to France and Sark. The islet on the right was once quarried for granite.

The harbour to Shell Beach via The Common

From the harbour take the path to the left, past the three island gift shops and Post Office. Here, old Herm stamps, now collectors items, are on sale. Major Wood ran an independent postal service between Herm and Guernsey early in his tenancy.

Look for the lamp post on the left, a legacy of the Perry era – painted blue, the colour of the Ford Motor Company logo.

The row of Mermaid Cottages were built in the early 1800s for quarrymen and their families and also housed British soldiers from a garrison based on the island during the First World War. The Tavern next door dates from Jonathan Duncan's era, and was once the site of a brewery and bakery.

The path leads on above Harbour Beach, and Fisherman's Beach. Fisherman's Cottage, on the right, was also built in the early 1800s – could it have been the home of the Hon Col. John Lindsay's mistress Mrs. Colebrook Cooper?

The small hill, Monku, rises up above the cottage. On the west side of the hill are scars from the time granite was hacked from the side of the hill. On the crest are neolithic graves.

A little further on is the island cemetery, the graves of two young men who probably died by drowning in the mid 1800s. Here the path divides – you can take a left over The Common, (once a nine hole golf links) or carry straight on towards Petit Monceau. A path climbs up and over the hill, and another winds round to the left. Mind the spiky marram grass and bramble bushes, although the walk is well worth the scratches.

At end of the path take a left for Oyster Point and a delightful secluded beach or right to cut across to Roberts Cross.

Walk ahead with Pierre Aux Rats in your sights and the path will take you above Oyster Beach, and then turning right, above North Beach. There are lovely views looking into the heart of the island, and to the left, out to sea.

Pierre Aux Rats was built to replace an ancient menhir demolished by quarrymen. The base of the obelisk is now covered in sand, evidence of the shifting dunes. Originally, the base once stood clear, about two feet high.

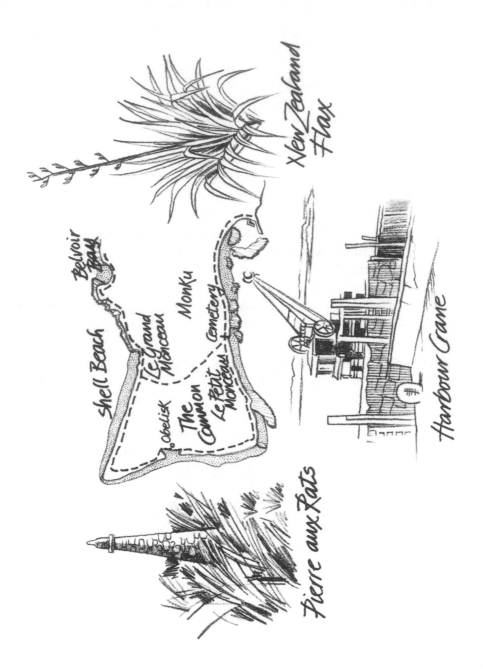

New Zealand Flax

Belvoir Bay

Shell Beach

Le Grand Monceau

Monku

Obelisk

The Common

Le Petit Monceau

Cemetery

Harbour Crane

Pierre aux Rats

A number of little paths lead down from the obelisk – take a left to cut across the common, covered in wind dried snail shells and dried rabbit bones. The path continues across open common and leads to another path above Shell Beach.

At the end of this path a sandy track to the right will take you back to Fisherman's Path, beneath the bracken covered Grand Monceau, site of a number of Neolithic tombs.

From Rosière to Shell Beach

The walk is quite hilly, there are numerous steps to negotiate and good walking shoes are recommended.

Three hours either side of low tide boats drop passengers off at the Rosière Steps, which lead through the granite arch, built during Prince Blücher's era as an entrance to the island.

A few steps beyond the arch is a pathway leading to the right up 15 steps. Look down from this position for an excellent view of the Rosière arch, and out across to the Pierre Percee reef with Jethou beyond.

The path climbs upwards, to a further set of eight steps, then levels out. In the spring the pathway is adorned with a variety of wild flowers. This pathway was hacked out during the Wood era. Before that bracken grew wild over the whole area.

The next flight of 29 steps results in magnificent views over Rosière and out to Jethou, with the two islets perched on either side of the island. In the distance lies Guernsey.

The path leads past sheer, bracken covered hillsides. On the right, hidden in the side of the hill is the entrance to an old silver mine, although there is no clear access. On the left, behind wired posts, is a ventilator shaft that drops down into the mine. Great care should be taken here.

Around the next corner enjoy a magnificent view of Sark. Stop awhile, sit among the boulders, and contemplate this lovely expanse of sea for this view alone is worth the walk.

The pathway from here shelves down, and can be slippery. Then, another flight of 29 steps – the Orr Steps – leads upwards to a further higher plateau, as the path weaves between fields on the left and a sheer drop on the right. In the spring puffins can be seen from here, as well as a host of other seabirds.

The first bay past the Orr Steps is where the Creux of Herm was situated, before it caved in. The next gully is Barbara's Leap, and yes she did leap from here.

As the path wends around a headland, look out for views on a fine day, across to France and to Alderney.

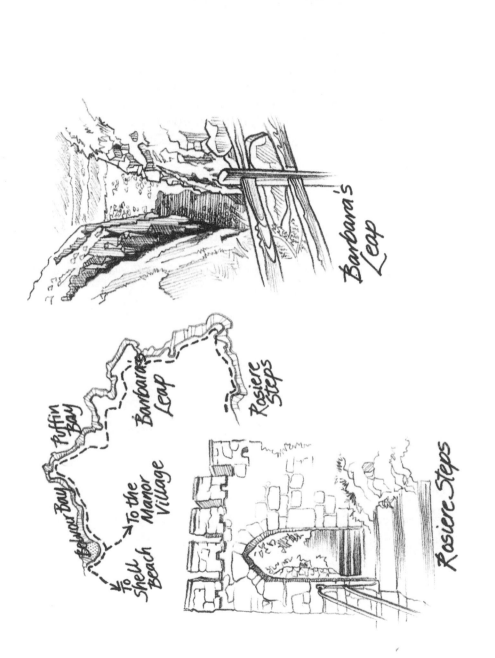

Barbara's Leap

Puffin Bay

Barbara's Leap

Rosiere Steps

To the Manor Village

Belvoir Bay

To Shell Beach

Rosiere Steps

At a junction the pathway to the left leads back to the Spine Road and the Manor Village. To continue take the fork to the right which has a lovely view over Puffin Bay, only accessible by sea. The large rock on the right is called Putrainez. From the next headland there are views ahead of Belvoir Bay and Shell Beach and this is a pleasant spot to sit and take a rest. The rock out to sea to the right is Caquorobert.

The pathway narrows for the final section to Belvoir Bay, and there are more steps to negotiate, this time downwards.

Follow the path past the bay and you are rewarded with a view out over Belvoir above the tops of sloe bushes. Around the next corner is one of the best views on Herm – Shell Beach stretches out in a shimmering golden line. On a clear day the yellow sand and sheer blue of the sea are quite breathtaking.

It is not far now to Shell Beach, where there is a café overlooking the beach. Now it's time to collect shells.